Evans Bell

The great parliamentary Bore

Evans Bell

The great parliamentary Bore

ISBN/EAN: 9783337151843

Printed in Europe, USA, Canada, Australia, Japan

Cover: Foto ©ninafisch / pixelio.de

More available books at **www.hansebooks.com**

THE GREAT PARLIAMENTARY BORE.

BY

MAJOR EVANS BELL,

LATE OF THE MADRAS STAFF CORPS.

AUTHOR OF "RETROSPECTS AND PROSPECTS OF INDIAN POLICY,"
" THE MYSORE REVERSION," ETC.

> " What, fifty followers?
> Is it not well? What should you need of more?
> Yea, or so many? sith that both charge and danger
> Speak 'gainst so great a number? How, in one house,
> Should many people, under two commands,
> Hold amity? 'Tis hard; almost impossible."
> SHAKESPEAR—*King Lear.*

LONDON:
TRÜBNER & CO., 60, PATERNOSTER ROW.
1869.

PREFACE.

If India, by common consent of all political parties, is a great Parliamentary bore, the greatest possible Parliamentary bore must surely be the case of Prince Azeem Jah. I have endeavoured to prove in this volume, that, bore as it may be, we must learn to deal manfully and directly with this particular affair of the Carnatic Sovereignty, and with the general affairs of our Indian Empire. If the British Parliament and people care for none of these things, and leave them much longer to the absolute will and pleasure of professional rulers, the ultimate result will be disastrous. The control of the Secretary of State, advised and instructed by a Council of retired officials, though salutary, is generally insufficient for the reversal of decrees to which the Department is committed. A Minister must be more or less tied by precedents and pledges. The Nation, when its eyes are opened, will never hold itself debarred from a thorough change of policy by any scruple of broken routine or inconsistent records, by reverence for the wisdom of a Lord Harris or a Lord Lyveden, or by any regard for the reputation or feelings of eminently respectable Peers in or out of office.

In the debate on Mr. Smollett's motion in favour of Prince Azeem Jah's claims, on the 13th of June, 1864, Mr. Lowe expressed an opinion that if cases of this description were to be brought before Parliament, after they had "slumbered for years," — "if such elements of uncertainty were allowed to be imported into the consideration of such questions,—there was danger of our Indian Empire being shaken to its foundation."*

The foundations of our Indian Empire will never be shaken by an act of justice. If Mr. Lowe himself, and those who have hitherto taken a similar view of the question, will have the patience to peruse the following pages to the end, they will see that this case has never "slumbered" for a year, or for a day; that it is very unlikely to slumber for many years, either in Parliament, or in India; and that "the elements of uncertainty" can no longer be hidden, and will never disappear, till the difference is finally settled on an intelligible basis, either by mutual agreement, or by fair arbitration.

It has been said, and will be said again, that the House of Commons is an unfit tribunal for the discussion and decision of such questions as these. It may be so, but at present there is no other tribunal. There is no Court of Appeal against what are called "acts of state."

Such of my readers as are not already acquainted with the Blue Books and the debates, will now have before them ample materials for satisfying themselves whether this important claim of succession to an inheritance is a fit subject for judicial inquiry, and whether it has ever received anything like judicial treatment or candid consideration. Let any one turn to the Papers of 1860, and ask himself whether he can imagine any barrister of decent character making use of the stuff he would find there, before the House of Lords or the Judicial Committee of Privy Council, addressing the Judges in the terms of Lord Harris's or Lord Dalhousie's Minutes. Yet no stronger advocacy has been employed, from first to last, to combat Prince Azeem Jah's claim. Every successive Governor of Madras, Governor-General and Secretary of State, since those iniquitous pleas were recorded, has manifestly shrunk from repeating them in his own name. After inordinate delays, the Prince has received no reply to his protest save a simple refusal of

---

* *Hansard*, vol. clxxv, p. 1668.

redress; and to this day the grounds alleged for his disinheritance have never been officially communicated to him. He has been left to find them out from the successive Blue Books that have been printed for public information.

Thus it is not merely a denial of redress that is complained of, but the positive denial of a hearing before an open Court, in a purely judicial matter. No possible remedy can be devised for the flagrant failure of justice in this, and other similar cases, still occasionally recurring, and always liable to recur, except the institution by law of some such tribunal as that suggested in the following extract from a Minute by Sir Bartle Frere, then a Member of the Governor's-General's Council, dated the 30th August, 1860.

"I trust I may not be misunderstood as saying a word against the right of appeal which every native of India ought to possess against any act of any Government functionary, however exalted. The exercise of such right of appeal will never, I am convinced, impair the true power of any Government of India such as we have had for generations past; and I trust the day is not far distant when the Sovereign may have at hand a tribunal forming a part of Her Majesty's Privy Council, or possessing the same relation to the Crown, which may at command sit in judgment on questions of executive administration, whether appealed from or referred by the Government of India, and which may decide such questions with an authority which shall be conclusive with Parliament and the public, as well as against any possible appellant."

"I believe that such a tribunal, advising the Crown on the exercise of its Sovereign prerogative on Indian matters, and of necessity excluding all irregular interference, would greatly strengthen the Government of India; but I am convinced that the present absence of system in dealing with Indian claims or Indian grievances in England, is fraught with great and immediate danger to the authority of Government, far beyond the admission of inconvenient burdens on our exhausted Treasury."*

The establishment of an Imperial judicature for the settlement of cases of disputed succession, of the doubtful interpretation of Treaties, and of other questions connected with the Princes of India beyond the province of municipal law, is the only cure for the well-intended iniquities of the Council-room, the inevitable scandals and

* *Papers, Mysore Family*, 1861, p. 121.

abuses of Parliamentary agency, or of agency still more irregular, the despairing intrigues of ruined royalty, the puzzled exasperation of faithful feudatories.

The knowledge that an appeal might be made to a competent Court would at once put our Governors and Councillors into a judicial frame of mind, so that very little room would be left for appeals, and very few appeals would lead to a reversal of the original decision. On the other hand, the appeal to an Imperial tribunal by a Sovereign Prince is a distinct act of submission to Imperial supremacy. In the appointment of such a tribunal there would be no loss of authority, and there would be an infinite gain of moral power.

CONTENTS.

Section	Pages
I.—As to Treaties and Titles	1 to 35
II.—As to Treachery and Treason	35 to 79
III.—Moral Results and Aspect	79 to 97
IV.—Professional Rule and its Organ	97 to 128
V.—Disinheritance and Defamation	128 to 146
VI.—Pillage and Malversation	146 to 155
VII.—An Inconclusive Conclusion	155 to 160
Postscript	161

APPENDIX.

A.—Sir Charles Wood's Despatch of the 8th April, 1862, (pp. 81, 95, 144, 149)	163
B.—Extract from the Private Journal of the Marquis of Hastings in 1813 (p. 129)	164
C.—Scindia's Famine Proclamation (p. 122)	166
D.—The Mysore Rajah's Private Accounts, (p. 127)	168
E.—Extracts from the *Times* and *Pall Mall Gazette*, (p. 154)	174
F.—The Treaties and an Opinion thereon	179

THE GREAT PARLIAMENTARY BORE.

THE claimant of the dignity and revenues of the Nawab of the Carnatic, whose case has been six times brought before the House of Commons within the last eight years,* is probably looked upon very generally not only as a very wearisome but as a very insignificant person, and many people would see nothing improper or inadequate in the description given of him during the debate of the 14th of March, 1865, by Mr. Vansittart, Member for Windsor, as "an individual who calls himself Prince Azeem Jah."† He is not regarded as a serious pretender, so much as an importunate pensioner, seeking to extort a larger stipend by a preposterous claim to sovereignty. Many who have a vague notion that the Prince and his family have been rather badly used, would yet acquiesce in the description of their status and of our relations with them, given by Sir Charles Wood (now Viscount Halifax) on the 26th of February, 1863, in the debate on Mr. H. J. Baillie's motion.

"The fact was that the Government of India in 1801 took possession of the territories of the Carnatic, and the then Nawab was reduced to the rank of a pensioner at Madras."

"The House therefore might dismiss at once all question of the annexation of territory."‡

* March 27th, 1860—Mr. Smollett's motion for papers.
July 25th, 1861—Mr. Layard's remarks.
February 26th, 1863—Right Hon. H. J. Baillie's motion.
July 7th, 1863—Sir Fitzroy Kelly's motion.
June 13th, 1864—Mr. Smollett's motion.
March 14th, 1865—Sir Fitzroy Kelly's motion.
† *Hansard*, vol. clxxvii, p. 1695.   ‡ *Ibid.*, vol. clxix, p. 814.

Yet no statement could well be more inaccurate. The East India Company certainly "took possession" of the Carnatic territories under the Treaty of 1801, in the same way as they "took possession" of Berar and other Provinces of the Nizam's Dominions under the Treaty of 1853,—for the purpose of "civil and military administration" and "exclusive management."* No annexation of territory took place on either occasion. Under the terms of those two Treaties, and after their completion, the successive Nawabs of the Carnatic, and the successive Nizams of the Deccan, retained, and were acknowledged by our Government to retain, the sovereignty of their territories, which we merely occupied and managed on certain conditions.

So far as the Nizam's Provinces of Berar are concerned, a published despatch from the Foreign Secretary at Calcutta to the Resident at Hyderabad, dated the 5th of September, 1860, tells us "that the Government of India desires to hold this territory, as it has hitherto held the whole of the Assigned Districts, not in sovereignty, but in trust for his Highness."†

The only distinction between the rights and interests of the Nizam and of the Nawab of the Carnatic respectively in their territorial possessions assigned by them to British management, is that while the "alienation" of the Nizam's districts is "temporary only" and "for a special purpose,"‡ "the sole and exclusive administration of the civil and military government" of the Carnatic territories, was "*for ever* vested in the East India Company," subject to the payment of a certain share of the revenues, "for the maintenance of the Nawab and the support of his dignity."§

We cannot, therefore, "dismiss all question of the annexation of territory" quite so summarily as Sir Charles

---

* See Article iv of the Treaty of 1801 with the Nawab Azeem-ood-Dowlah of the Carnatic, (*Collection of Treaties*, Calcutta, 1864, Longmans, London, vol. v, p. 250) and compare with Article vi of the Treaty of 1853 with the Nizam, (*Collection of Treaties*, vol. v, pp. 104-5.)
† *Papers, the Deccan.* 1867, p. 20. ‡ *Ibid.*, 1867, p. 20.
§ *Collection of Treaties*, vol. v, p. 250.

Wood desires. If the Carnatic territories are ours, they must have been annexed at some distinguishable period, and by some intelligible process. When did that annexation take place ? By his assertion that " the Nawab was reduced to the rank of a pensioner at Madras in 1801," Sir Charles Wood apparently fixes the annexation in that year. It will not be difficult to show that he is quite mistaken.

We know that the Nawab of the Carnatic retained the sovereignty of his territories after the conclusion of the Treaty of 1801, negatively, because that Treaty contains no form of cession, of relinquishment or transfer of sovereignty ; positively, because the sovereignty of the Nawab who concluded that Treaty, and of his successors, was always asserted by themselves, and repeatedly acknowledged and proclaimed in plain terms by the other contracting party, the British Government, down to the year 1855.

Sir Charles Wood said that in 1801 " the Nawab was reduced to the rank of a pensioner at Madras."* This is in direct contradiction not only to the letter and spirit of the Treaty and other public documents of 1801, but to the explanatory statements made at the time by the highest authorities in India and England.

Lord Clive, the Governor of Madras, describing the successful conclusion of the Treaty to the Governor General, Lord Wellesley, in a despatch dated the 27th of July, 1801, writes as follows :—

"This mode of arrangement, while it cannot encroach upon our security, is calculated to qualify the entire transfer of *the civil government* of the Carnatic to the hands of the British, with the preservation of an active principle *for securing an union of interests between the Nawab of the Carnatic and the Company in the administration of the affairs of the country.*"†

And in his despatch of the 3rd of August, 1801, to the Secret Committee of the Court of Directors, he says :— " The mode of supplying a fund for the expenses of *the*

---

* *Ante*, p. 1. † *Asiatic Annual Register*, 1802, p. 155.

family" "is entirely relieved from the degrading name and appearance of *a stipendiary maintenance.*"*

The Marquis Wellesley, by whom the Treaty of 1801 was ratified, in a despatch dated the 18th of August, 1801, writes as follows to the Governor of Madras :— "His Excellency in Council highly approves the consideration which has been manifested for the prejudices and condition of his Highness as the acknowledged Soubadar of Arcot, *in apportioning his income on the revenues of the Carnatic, rather than by granting it in the form of a pension.*"†

By innumerable public declarations and engagements the ancestors of Prince Azeem Jah were acknowledged by our Government as hereditary Sovereigns. Whatever lands and revenues the East India Company held within the limits of the Carnatic they held by grant or assignment from the Nawab as Sovereign. The struggle for predominancy in Southern India between the English and the French was terminated by the Treaty of Paris in 1763, under Article XI of which both Governments agreed to recognise Mahomed Ali Wallajah, Prince Azeem Jah's great-grandfather, as "legitimate Nawab of the Carnatic."‡ The British Government hailed that recognition, which it had cost great pains to gain, "as a confirmation of our title to the territories we hold under grants," and as an establishment of our Ally, the Nawab, in "the sovereignty of the Carnatic."§

The Nawab Azeem-ood-Dowlah, father of Prince Azeem Jah, was established by the Treaty of 1801 "in the rank, property, and possessions of his ancestors, heretofore Nawabs of the Carnatic."|| His position therefore was that of hereditary Sovereign. And by numerous public acts subsequent to that Treaty, the British Government pronounced the sovereignty and feudal supremacy of the

---

* *Carnatic Papers*, 1861, p. 108. † *Ibid.*, 1861, p. 110.
‡ *Martens, Recueil des Traités*, etc., tome i, p. 113.
§ *Asiatic Annual Register*, vol. x, 1808, p. 495.
|| See Preamble and Article i of the Treaty, *Collection of Treaties*, Calcutta, 1864, (Longmans, London) vol. v, p. 248, 249 ; and *Carnatic Papers*, 1861, p. 113.

Nawab to be unchanged, undisturbed and undiminished, although he had thereby divested himself of all executive power.

Here is an extract of a letter from the Madras Government to the Court of Directors, dated 17th February, 1802 :—

"Having received from the Resident at Travancore an application on the part of the Rajah requesting to be made acquainted with the channel through which his stipulated annual payments were in future to be made *to his immediate superior Lord*, we directed his Excellency to be informed that the Peshcush, nuzzuranahs, and nuzzurs payable by his Excellency were to be transmitted according to the ancient usage, to the Durbar of the Nabob of the Carnatic."*

And in a letter from the Governor of Madras to the Court of Directors, dated the 22nd February 1803, it is said :—

"We have the honour to inform you that, conformably to the principle already explained to your Honourable Court, the Rajah of Travancore has paid to his Highness the Nabob, *as the Sovereign of the Carnatic*, the sum of 2266 pagodas and 15 annas, in full discharge of the Peishcush and Cape Comorin Nuzzurana, due to his Highness for the preceding Phuzly."†

A Declaration was issued by the Government of Madras on the 1st February, 1803, to the following effect :—

"We, the undersigned, the Governor in Council of Fort St. George, do hereby certify that the Nabob Wallajah Azeem-oodDowlah, Soubadar of the Carnatic, is acknowledged and recognised by our said Government as an independent Prince, the Soubadar of the Carnatic Payen Ghaut, and an Ally of our said Government."‡

In this document the Nawab Azeem-ood-Dowlah is represented as occupying exactly the same position as his predecessors since the year 1768, "being successively Soubadars of the Carnatic and Allies of the Government," and as "now residing near Madras," "for the purpose of carrying on, in concert with the Government of Fort St. George, the common and united interests of the said Government,

---

* *Carnatic Papers*, 1861, p. 118.   † *Ibid.*, 1861, p. 127.
‡ *Ibid.*, 1861, p. 126.

and of the said several successive Soubadars of the Carnatic Payen Ghaut, as such Allies."* A stipendiary or pensioner could not be declared to be "an independent Prince" and "an Ally," or described as acting "in concert with the British Government" on behalf of their "common and united interests."

Three years after the Treaty of 1801 another Governor of Madras, Lord William Bentinck, writes to the Nawab Azeem-ood-Dowlah in the following terms :—

"The Government was pleased to establish your Highness *upon the throne*, reserving to itself the administration of the civil and military affairs of the country ; a very considerable portion of the revenue was appropriated to the support of the rank and dignity of *the Sovereign* in his former splendour."†

Nine years later the Court of Directors write as follows :—

"It appears from the report of the Advocate-General, of the 22nd of September, 1810, that the rights of His Highness the Nabob *as a Sovereign Prince* have been allowed and confirmed by the Supreme Court of Judicature, and declared to be exempt from its local jurisdiction."‡

Even under the terms of the Treaty of 1801, by which executive authority was transferred to the East India Company, a certain consultative share in the Government is still reserved for the Native Sovereign. By Article IX the Company is charged with the maintenance of some collateral branches of the Wallajah family, and it is stipulated that "the amount of the above-mentioned expenses, to be defrayed by the Company, shall be distributed, *with the knowledge of the Nawab, in such manner as shall be judged proper.*" By the First Separate Explanatory Article it is provided that "whenever the whole net revenue of the Carnatic shall exceed the sum of twenty-five lakhs of Star Pagodas, the fifth part of such surplus

---

* *Carnatic Papers*, 1861, p. 126.

† Letter from Lord W. Bentinck to the Nawab Azeem-ood-Dowlah, dated the 22nd May, 1804; *Papers relating to Carnatic Stipendiaries*, Madras, 1858, pp. 97-98.

‡ From the Court of Directors to the Government of Madras, dated 23rd of February, 1813 ; *Carnatic Stipendiaries*, Madras, 1858, p. 138.

shall be applied to the repair of fortifications, to the establishment of a separate fund for the eventful exigencies of war, or to the military defence of the Carnatic, in such manner as may be determined by the Governor in Council of Fort St. George, *after previous communication to His Highness the Nawab Azeem-ood-Dowlah.*"*

It was by this ingenious Explanatory Article that Lord Wellesley contrived to transform the Nawab's fifth share of the revenue into an income practically fixed, which might, indeed, fall with a declining revenue, but would not be allowed to rise with any improvement in the public resources. But in his despatch on the subject, dated the 18th of August, 1801, (paragraph 19) Lord Wellesley desires that "the proposed restriction should be made in a manner the less unacceptable to the feelings and injurious to the rank of the Nawab. With this view his Excellency proposes that, in restricting the extreme amount of his Highness's income, it should be expressly declared that the surplus of revenue beyond the amount which shall yield to his Highness the full extent of his limited income, is to be appropriated to the purpose of establishing a fund for the contingency of war, or for any other public purpose which it may be thought expedient to specify. His Excellency in Council accordingly directs that an Explanatory Article be framed in terms conformable to the foregoing observations."†

The consultative share in the Government of the Carnatic conceded to the Nawab, was doubtless intended to be merely nominal and complimentary, just enough to soften the asperities and disguise the restrictions of the Treaty. But the introduction of such provisions is only one among the many conclusive proofs that the Nawab was not reduced by the Treaty of 1801, as Sir Charles Wood asserted, "to the rank of a pensioner at Madras,"‡ and that his territories were not annexed under that Treaty.

The broad assertion that in 1801 the Nawab was re-

* *Collection of Treaties*, vol. v, pp. 252, 255, and *Carnatic Papers*, 1861, pp. 104 and 113.
† *Carnatic Papers*, 1861, p. 110   ‡ *Ante*, p. 1.

duced to "the rank of a pensioner at Madras," might pass muster in a speech at the end of a debate in the House of Commons, but could not be deliberately recorded in writing. We find it in none of the published Minutes or despatches. More elaborate efforts are there put forth to neutralise and annul the effect of the Treaty of 1801. Lord Harris, who was Governor of Madras when the late Nawab died, argued that this Treaty "containing no provision for a successor, no mention being made of successors," is a mere "personal" treaty, applying only to the individual Prince with whom it was contracted, and terminable at his demise.* These views, in which Lord Dalhousie and the Court of Directors concurred,† rest upon two gross and palpable errors, which would have been dispelled at once if a reference had been made for the opinion of any eminent authority in International Law. The first error is that a Treaty becomes a "personal" Treaty, if it is made with a Prince by name, and does not contain the words "heirs and successors." The second error is that the meaning of the term "personal Treaty," is a Treaty made for one life only.

The fact is that a Treaty might contain the words, "heirs and successors," in every Article and clause, and yet be a "personal" Treaty, while the absence of those words from a Treaty does not in the least detract from the perpetuity of its obligations on both sides. Grotius points out that it is not necessary that the words "heirs and successors" "should be introduced in order to make the Treaty real."‡

A "personal" Treaty is not a Treaty made for one life only, but a Treaty made for the private objects and interests of a Prince or *family*, and to last only as long as the person or *the family* lasts. It has no direct reference to the interests of the State or people, but only to those of the King or *dynasty*, and expires with them. Even an undoubted "personal" Treaty would not expire, for want of the words, "heirs and successors," at the death

---

* *Carnatic Papers*, 1860, pp. 12, 13.   † *Ibid.*, pp. 47, 48, and 45.
‡ *De Jure Belli et Pacis*, lib. ii, c. xv.

of the individual named in it, if its evident object was to secure certain advantages to his family.

The Treaty of 1801, as I shall show, is manifestly a "real" Treaty, but if it were a "personal" Treaty, it would remain in force as long as any member of the Wallajah family existed.

> "Treaties, properly so called, are either *personal* or *real*. They are personal, when their continuation in force depends on the person of the Sovereign, *(or his family)*, with whom they have been contracted. They are real, when their duration depends on the State, independently of the person who contracts. All treaties made for a time specified, or for ever, are also real."*

Wheaton, perhaps the greatest of modern authorities, writes as follows on the same subject:—

> "Treaties are divided into *personal* and *real*. The former relate exclusively to the persons of the contracting parties, such as family alliances, and treaties guaranteeing the throne to a particular Sovereign and his family. They expire, of course, on the death of the King, *or the extinction of his family*."†

The Wallajah family is not extinct. A son of the particular Sovereign with whom the Treaty of 1801 was contracted, now claims the benefit of its provisions.

If it were a "personal" Treaty, the right of Prince Azeem Jah, and the representative of the Wallajah family "for ever," "in all time to come," to succeed, under its terms, to the state and rank of Nawab of the Carnatic, and to the stipulated share of the revenue, would be absolute. But the tenour and spirit of the Treaty throughout stamp it as a "real" Treaty. Grotius says:—"If it be added to the Treaty that *it shall stand for ever*, or that it is made *for the good of the Kingdom*, it will from hence fully appear that the Treaty is *real*."‡

The Treaty of 1801 is made "to establish the connection between the contracting parties *on a permanent basis of security in all times to come*,"§ which is much the same as saying that "it shall stand for ever."

---

* *Law of Nations*, translated from G. F. Von Martens, London, 1803, p. 54.   † *Elements of International Law*, Boston, 1855, p. 39.
‡ *De Jure Belli et Pacis*, lib. ii, cap. 16. See also Vattel, paragraphs 187, 189.   § Preamble, (*Collection of Treaties*, vol. v, pp. 248, 249.

The Treaty of 1801 is made for "the entire defence of the Carnatic against foreign enemies, and the maintenance of the internal tranquillity and police of the country,"*— which is much the same as saying that "it is made for the good of the Kingdom." According to the definitions of Grotius and Vattel, therefore, the Treaty of 1801 is a "real" Treaty.

But in fact the Treaty of 1801 does not stand alone. It declares itself to be inseparably bound up with the previous Treaties between the East India Company and the Nawabs of the Carnatic. Those of 1787 and 1792 are specially cited as not having entirely "fulfilled the intention of *the contracting parties*," and the new Treaty is said to contain "*additional* provisions," and to "be made for the purpose of *supplying the defects of all former engagements.*"† It is, in fact, a supplementary engagement. The recital of the previous Treaties as having "been intended to identify the interests of *the contracting parties;*" the statement that "the intentions of *the contracting parties* have not been fulfilled by any of the Treaties heretofore concluded;" and finally the declaration that the new Treaty, with its "additional provisions," is to "supply the defects of all former engagements and to establish the connection between *the contracting parties on a permanent basis of security in all times to come,*" manifestly denote as "*the contracting parties,*" the representatives of the Wallajah family, and of the East India Company, in the past, in the present, and in the future, and provide for a perpetual alliance and a perpetual succession on both sides.

The Preamble of the Treaty of 1801 announces that "the Prince Azeem-ood-Dowlah has been established by the English East India Company *in the rank, property, and possessions of his ancestors,* heretofore Nawabs of the Carnatic;" and Article I that he is established "*in the state and rank, with the dignities dependent thereon, of his ancestors,* heretofore Nawabs of the Carnatic." Article II of this Treaty expressly "*confirms and renews such*

---

* Article xi, (*Collection of Treaties,* vol. v, p. 252.)
† Preamble (*Collection of Treaties,* vol. v, p. 249.)

parts of the Treaties heretofore concluded between the East India Company and their Highnesses, heretofore Nabobs of the Carnatic, as are calculated to strengthen the alliance, to cement the friendship, and to identify the interests of the contracting parties." The Third Article speaks of "*reviving the fundamental principles of the alliance*" between the Nawab's "ancestors and the English nation."* The former Treaties contain ample guaranties of succession to the Nawab Wallajah's heirs.† The Treaty of 1801 confirms all such parts of former Treaties as were favourable and friendly to the Nawab. Therefore the guaranties of hereditary succession, the essential principle of the Sovereign rank and dignity of his ancestors, are, as among the most important of the favourable and friendly conditions of former Treaties, effectually renewed and confirmed by the Treaty of 1801.

This document is pervaded by a superabundance of conditions and expressions that prove our Government to have dealt with Prince Azeem Jah's father as a Sovereign and not as a stipendiary.

"The friends and enemies of either are the friends and enemies of both parties."

"The Honourable Company charges itself with the maintenance and support of the military force necessary for the defence of the Carnatic, and for the protection of the rights, person and property of the Nawab Azeem-ood-Dowlah."

"The Nawab Azeem-ood-Dowlah agrees that he will not enter upon any negociation or correspondence with any European or Native Power, without the knowledge and consent of the said English Company."‡

These are not exactly the terms that would be used in dealing with a stipendiary. The Nawab is repeatedly styled "an Ally," and the relation between him and the East India Company is described as an "alliance."§

Before the death of the late Nawab in 1855,—when Lord Dalhousie wrote from the Neilgherry Hills to Lord

* *Collection of Treaties,* vol. v, p. 249.
† See Preamble to the Treaty of 1792, (*Collection of Treaties,* vol. v, pp. 236, 237.)
‡ *Collection of Treaties,* vol. v, pp. 251, 252.
§ Preamble, Articles ii, iii, v, x, of Treaty of 1801, (*Collection of Treaties,* vol. v, pp. 248, 252.)

Harris at Madras that there was *no direct heir to the Musnud*,"*—no doubt as to the hereditary nature of the Nawab's dignity had ever been expressed or hinted at by any British authority. Two successions had taken place since the Treaty of 1801. Three generations, father, son, and grandson, had occupied the throne. Neither the phrase nor the idea of "a personal Treaty,"—of binding force only during the life of the first of these three,—can be found in the transactions of any Governor of Madras or Governor-General, from Lord Wellesley down to Lord Hardinge.

In a Memorandum drawn up in 1806 by the Duke of Wellington, (then Sir Arthur Wellesley) as materials for a Parliamentary defence of his brother, the Marquis Wellesley, it is expressly stated that the Treaty of 1801 was concluded so that "the civil and military government of the Carnatic was transferred for ever to the Company; and the Nabob Azeem-ood-Dowlah, *and his heirs*, were to preserve their title and dignity and to receive one-fifth part of the net revenues of the country."† Prince Azeem Jah is a son of the Nawab Azeem-ood-Dowlah.

The anticipated discussion on the Carnatic transactions of 1801, amounting to a proposed vote of censure on the Marquis Wellesley, took place at last in 1808. During the whole course of the debate no one, whether a supporter or an opponent of Lord Wellesley's policy, suggested that under the Treaty of 1801 the hereditary dignity of the Wallajah family was impaired, or endangered, or left to the "grace and favour" of the British Government.‡

The best possible contemporary explanation of the objects and intentions of our Government, may naturally be sought in the writings of Lord Clive,§ who negotiated the Treaty of 1801 under the instructions of Lord Welles-

---

* *Carnatic Papers*, 1860, p. 17.
† *Supplementary Despatches of the Duke of Wellington*, vol. iv, pp. 564, 565.
‡ *Hansard's Debates*, vol. xi, pp. 315, 767, 921.
§ The second Lord Clive, afterwards Earl of Powis, then Governor of Madras.

ley, and in constant communication with him, and who remained Governor of Madras for two years after the Treaty was concluded. Everything recorded by him on the subject directly contradicts the notions first conceived by Lords Dalhousie and Harris in 1855, that the Nawab's dignity ceased to be hereditary in 1801, that Azeem-ood-Dowlah was only a life-tenant under the new Treaty, that the rights of the Wallajah family were annihilated, and that they were thenceforward entirely dependent on the "grace and favour" of the East India Company.

In a despatch to the Governor-General dated the 27th of July, 1801, reporting the successful conclusion of the Treaty, Lord Clive describes it as "the gracious and conciliatory measure of establishing *a branch of the House of Mahomed Ali* in a degree of rank and splendour suitable to *its long subsisting connection with the Company.*"*

In a despatch dated the 3rd of August, 1801, to the Secret Committee of the Court of Directors, Lord Clive writes as follows :—

"In conformity to this arrangement we have acknowledged Azeem-ood-Dowlah to be Nawab of the Carnatic. The mode of providing for the support of the dignity of His Highness is conformable to the principles on which the alliance between *His Highness's family* and the Company has been *revived and established.*"†

On the 18th December 1801, a circular issued by Lord Clive to all the members of the Nawab's family explains to them that the new arrangement was made—"to preserve to that respectable *family* its ancient rank among the Princes of Hindostan," and "that when the Nawab Azeem-ood-Dowlah was raised to the rank of Nawab of the Carnatic, his Highness *succeeded to the rights of his illustrious ancestors heretofore* Nawabs of the Carnatic." How is it possible that the ancient rank of the family could be preserved by means of a mere life Treaty with the Nawab Azeem-ul-Dowlah? In the same document he speaks of the "restored alliance," and of the "rank and dignity of this illustrious *family*," and says that "the alliance is now firmly and *perpetually* established."‡ How

* *Carnatic Papers*, 1861, p. 101. † *Ibid.*, p. 108.
‡ *Ibid.* pp. 118, 119.

could an alliance be "perpetually" established by means of a Treaty that was good for one life only?

Some who defend the action of our Government in this matter have, however, asserted that the Nawabs of the Carnatic after 1801 were merely "nominal" or "titular" Sovereigns, and "virtual" pensioners, and that they were justly reduced to that condition in consequence of the treachery and violation of former Treaties of which the Nawabs Mahomed Ali Wallajah and Omdut-ool-Oomra were convicted.

A very short and sufficient answer to these offensive imputations, when brought forward to disparage Prince Azeem Jah's claims, is that even granting the alleged perfidy was proved,—on which we shall have a few words to say,—the full penalty was exacted in 1801 by our forcing upon Azeem-ood-Dowlah a new Treaty, by which he resigned the exercise of sovereign power beyond the precincts of his Palace, and accepted a certain share of the revenues of his Principality for the maintenance of himself and his family. All that Lord Wellesley required was the perpetual transfer of the "civil and military administration," which Wallajah and Omdut-ool-Oomra, relying on the rights secured to them by the Treaty of 1792, had pertinaciously refused to resign, and which Lord Wellesley persuaded himself he was justified in exacting as the condition of the renewal of friendly relations with their successor. That was the extent of Lord Wellesley's demands, and that was the extent of the penalty inflicted on the Wallajah family by the Treaty of 1801.

Lord Harris proposes to make a "reference to the intentions and opinions of those, viz., Lord Wellesley and Lord Clive, who framed the Treaty of 1801. Nothing can be clearer," continues Lord Harris, "than Lord Wellesley's views *on this subject*." (Would not any one suppose that "*this subject*" was the Treaty of 1801?) "In writing to Mr. Dundas, he says, 'The whole question of succession will therefore be completely open to the decision of the Company upon the decease of the present Nawab.'"*

* *Carnatic Papers*, 1860, p. 10; *Wellesley's Despatches*, vol. ii, p. 244.

Lord Harris seems to have overlooked the fact that this despatch to Mr. Dundas was written on the 5th of March, 1800, more than a year before the Treaty of 1801 was concluded. "The present Nawab" therein mentioned was not Azeem-ood-Dowlah with whom the Treaty was made, but Omdut-ool-Oomra, whose death was almost daily expected; and in saying that "the question of the succession would be completely open upon the decease of the Nawab," Lord Wellesley was alluding to the magnanimous plan of provoking a disputed succession, and imposing our own terms, as the price of our support, upon the more compliant candidate.

It is quite true that Lord Wellesley, as Lord Harris observes, "appears to have wavered as to which policy to pursue,—whether to allow the continuance of a Nawab, or to assume the *nominal* as well as the real sovereignty in the name of the Company."* Here are Lord Wellesley's own words:—

"It will be expedient that you should immediately consider whether it might not be a more effectual arrangement to provide liberally for every branch of the descendants of Wallajah and Omdut-ool-Oomra, and to vest even the nominal sovereignty of the Carnatic in the Company. No doubt exists in my mind that the British Government would now be completely justified in depriving the Nawab of all power over his country, and reducing him to the state of a mere pensioner."†

These are the words that probably misled Sir Charles Wood. But Lord Wellesley penned these lines, and "wavered as to which policy to pursue," in March 1800. The Treaty was concluded on the 31st July, 1801. In the interval Lord Wellesley had ceased to waver. Although he had perfected the happy expedient of charging the Nawabs with treachery, and had carefully arranged the most effectual machinery for applying the superior force of the British Government to "deprive the Nawab of all power over his country," Lord Wellesley wavered no longer in 1801, as to the exact limits of that deprivation. He decided that it would *not* be politic, and was not, in-

* *Carnatic Papers*, 1860, p. 11.
† *Wellesley's Despatches*, vol. ii, p. 244,—*Carnatic Papers*, 1860, p. 10.

deed, practicable, to "reduce the Nawab to the state of a mere pensioner," or "to vest the nominal sovereignty of the Carnatic in the Company."

The strong expressions used by Lord Wellesley while his mind was yet undecided as to the best course to pursue, are adduced by Lords Dalhousie and Harris, and by those who support the transactions of 1855, as if they represented the course that he actually did pursue.

Lord Wellesley in several despatches on the subject of the new Treaty, makes use of language similar to that finally embodied in the public Declaration issued, under his instructions, by the Governor of Madras, dated the 31st of July, 1801, explaining that " by their hostile and faithless conduct" the deceased Nawabs Wallajah and Omdut-ool-Oomra had " placed themselves in the relation of public enemies with the British Empire," had "forfeited all the benefits of their alliance with the Company," and had "annihilated the vital spirit of the Treaty of 1792." It goes on to say that at the death of the Nawab Omdut-ool-Oomra, " the British Government remained at liberty to exercise its rights, founded on the faithless policy of its Ally, in whatever manner might be deemed most conducive to the immediate safety and the general interests of the Company in the Carnatic."*

The question for us to consider now is, not what the British Government was "at liberty" to do, or what it *might* have done, but what actually was done. And this we learn from that same Declaration. The British Government determined to adhere "to the principles of moderation and forbearance," and to make " an amicable adjustment."

" The British Government, still adhering to the principles of moderation, and actuated by its uniform desire of obtaining security for its rights and interests in the Carnatic, by an arrangement founded *on the principles of the long subsisting alliance between the Company and the family of the Nawab Mahomed Ali*, judged it expedient to enter into a negociation for that purpose with the Prince Azeem-ood-Dowlah, the son and heir of Ameer-ool-Oomra, who was the second son of the Nawab Mahomed Ali,

---

* *Wellesley's Despatches*, vol. ii, p. 5.

and the immediate great-grandson by both parents of the Nawab Anwar-ood-deen Khan of blessed memory. And his Highness, Prince Azeem-ood-Dowlah Bahadoor, having entered into engagements for the express purpose of reviving the alliance between the Company and his illustrious ancestors, and of establishing an adequate security for the British interests in the Carnatic, the British Government has now resolved to exercise its rights and its power, under Providence, in supporting and establishing the hereditary pretensions of the Prince Azeem-ood-Dowlah Bahadoor, in the Soubadary of the Carnatic."*

There were good and sufficient reasons for Lord Wellesley having decided between March 1800 and May 1801, that he must not attempt to annex the Carnatic, to reduce the Nawab to the position of a pensioner, or to deprive him of the sovereignty. Such an act of usurpation and violence at that critical period, when the more important Native States were observing with alarm and jealousy the increased stability and mobility of our power in consequence of the downfall of Tippoo Sultan's Kingdom, and while a formidable revolt raged in the Carnatic itself, might have excited a combination against our Government that would have taxed our resources to the utmost, would certainly have ruined our finances, and might have led to a great disaster. Here are Lord Wellesley's own words in a letter to Lord Clive of the 4th of June, 1801.

" It is by no means certain that, in the event of our proceeding to exercise a right founded on a violation of Treaty, and on the necessity of self-defence, *the Powers of Hindostan would refrain from confounding the abstract principles of the general law of nations with ambitious views of aggrandisement and extension of dominion.*"†

Immediately after the conclusion of the new Treaty, Lord Clive writes on the 27th July 1801 to Calcutta, stating that

" The rebellion in the Southern Provinces has assumed a more formidable aspect than could have been expected, and has so reduced the appointed force of the Provinces *as to render extremely inconvenient any measure calculated to augment the number of disaffected persons.*"

* *Wellesley's Despatches*, vol. ii, p. 560.
† *Ibid.*, vol. ii, p. 535; *Carnatic Papers*, 1861, p. 96

"Every consideration of our general policy of expediency *with respect to our external relations, and of prudence with regard to our internal tranquillity*, requires, in my judgment, that the actual establishment of our security, on the basis of right to exercise the entire civil and military government of the Carnatic, should be accompanied by the gracious and conciliatory measure of *establishing a branch of the House of Mahomed Ali* in a degree of rank and splendour suited to its long subsisting connection with the Company."*

In another despatch of the same date as that we have just quoted, Lord Clive reported to the Governor-General that "considering the actual state of affairs, the inefficient and dispersed state of our military force at this Presidency, and what it has to perform, as well as *the precarious and unpleasant situation of domestic politics*," he had decided on "the expediency of obtaining an effectual control over the Carnatic by negociation, if practicable, rather than by assumption by force," and he described the Treaty which he submitted for Lord Wellesley's judgment, as "a transaction which places Azeem-ood-Dowlah on the musnud and *the control* of the Carnatic in the Company."†

In addition to the jealous hostility of several Native Powers, which at last exploded in the Mahratta war of 1803, when we were less encumbered and better prepared, "the situation of domestic politics" in the Carnatic in 1801, was, as Lord Clive said, "precarious and unpleasant." The rebellion of the Southern Chieftains,—the Polygar war, as it was called,—was carried on most obstinately; and some of the most desperate fighting took place about the time that the scheme for depriving the Nawab of power was being finally settled in correspondence between Lord Clive and the Marquis Wellesley.

The little Fort of Punjalum-coorchy in the Tinnevelly district, was attacked on the 31st March, 1801, by a force under Major Macaulay, consisting of two Companies of the 74th Foot and five Native Battalions; and although the defenders are said to have been armed for the most part with pikes, the attack completely failed, with a loss on our side of 17 officers and 74 European soldiers, and 229

---

* *Carnatic Papers*, 1861, pp. 100, 101.
† *Wellesley's Despatches*, vol. ii, p. 552.

Sepoys, killed and wounded. Reinforcements having arrived to the extent of a Company of Artillery with six guns, a Regiment of Cavalry, the 77th Foot and two more Native Battalions, the place was stormed with success on the 23rd of May, 1801. The storming party was formed of four Companies of Europeans, (two of the 74th, two of the 77th) and eight Companies of Sepoys; and their loss in one hour's hard fighting amounted to 9 officers and 95 Europeans, (or about one in three of those engaged) and 120 Sepoys, killed and wounded. Upwards of 450 of the enemy were killed inside the Fort, which is described by a very competent eye-witness, who was present at the assault, as "a mere dog-kennel."[*]

Nor was the progress of this Polygar war watched with indifference by the Government of India. It was well understood that such untoward incidents as the failure before Punjalum-coorchy might lead to a most unpleasant crisis. Henry Wellesley writing from the Governor-General's household at Calcutta to Colonel Arthur Wellesley at Bombay, on the 22nd of April, 1801, says:—

"I am sorry to tell you that we have met with a great loss in the Tinnevelly country against the Fort of Punjalum-coorchy; —upwards of 300 men killed and wounded, and the Fort not taken."[†]

The affair evidently made a considerable impression on the future Duke, for in a letter dated the 28th of the same month, from Cannanore on the Western Coast, to the Governor of Bombay, he gives the following account of it, from which we gather some additional details:—

"The Polygars in the Southern Provinces of the Carnatic have contended most successfully, as I am informed, against a detachment of our troops under Major Macaulay. It is said that he lost, in some attack which he made on Punjalum-coorchy Fort, above 70 out of two Companies of Europeans, and about 250

---

[*] *General Welsh's Military Reminiscences*, (Smith and Elder, 1830) vol. i, pp. 62 to 78. This almost forgotten affair of Punjalum-coorchy, with others that might be adduced in a chain coming down to the year 1846, may serve to dispel a very prevalent notion that the only warlike races in India are to be found in the North. Aurungzebe found out his mistake of despising the Mahrattas.

[†] *Wellington's Supplementary Despatches*, vol. ii, p. 364.

Sepoys out of five Battalions, and failed to carry the Fort. The Polygars assembled and attacked his camp in the night, and his detachment on their march on the next day but one, and on both occasions were repulsed with difficulty and with some loss on our side."

"The detachment in the Southern Division of the Carnatic has been reinforced by the 77th Regiment from Malabar, and by other troops from different parts."*

On the 21st of June, 1801—very near the time when the death of the Nawab Omdut-ool-Oomra, then daily expected,† was to compel the immediate settlement of the succession and the new Treaty,—Arthur Wellesley writes from Seringapatam to Sir David Baird as follows :—

"To the Southward matters have been going on very badly indeed."

He then gives a full account of the first unsuccessful assault on Punjalum-coorchy, mentioning the names of several officers who were killed and wounded, and continues thus :—

"The Fort has since been attacked and carried, with much loss on our side and great slaughter of the Polygars. The head Polygar escaped, and he has been joined by others in the Southern countries, and even by the Colleries, all of them excited to insurrection by the misfortunes of our troops at the commencement of the contest. Within these few days they have again opposed the troops in the open field, and, I am informed, have stood with great firmness, and that the result of the contest, although favourable to us, was not unattended by loss on our side. Upon this last occasion Major Grey of the Company's Service was killed, and other officers were wounded. Colonel Agnew has been again reinforced by troops from all quarters; but it appears to be the general opinion of those best acquainted with the people with whom the contest was sustained, and with the country which is its seat, that it will be tedious and unpleasant."

"Besides this warfare to the Southward, there is one going on in the Northern Circars, with the details of which I am unacquainted."‡

---

* *Wellington's Supplementary Despatches*, vol. ii, p. 369.

† He died on the 15th of July; the new Treaty was signed on the 21st.

‡ *Wellington's Supplementary Despatches*, vol. ii, pp. 460, 461.

At such a time as this Lord Clive might well say that "any measure calculated to augment the number of disaffected persons would be extremely inconvenient."* The revolt of the Southern Polygars might have assumed unexpected proportions, and have led to unforeseen complications, if a pretender to the Carnatic musnud had placed himself at its head. By installing a Nawab, concluding a Treaty with him, proclaiming his succession to the throne "*by the hereditary rights of his father,*" and calling on "all the Zemindars, Jaghiredars, Talookdars, Polygars, officers and inhabitants of the Carnatic," to "yield due obedience to the orders of the Company," "*by virtue of the rights and powers acquired by compact with the present lawful Nawab,*"† the Governor of Madras checkmated the more active and ambitious members and adherents of the Wallajah family, and left them without any available rallying point.

We have already quoted from the Declaration circulated by our Government in 1801 a passage stating that "the hereditary pretensions of Prince Azeem-ood-Dowlah had been supported and established."‡ Besides this, the Proclamation issued by the Government on the 31st of July, 1801, to the Zemindars and people of the Carnatic, expressly states that Azeem-ood-Dowlah "has succeeded by the *hereditary rights* of his father, and by full acknowledgment of the Honourable Company, to the possession of the said Musnud."§

Notwithstanding these unequivocal expressions in documents published at the time, Lord Harris ventures on the following extraordinary statement:—

"Azeem-ood-Dowla was positively and openly declared to have no hereditary claims."‖

What was "positively and openly declared" was the very reverse of this. Lord Wellesley did, indeed, secretly and confidentially intimate something of the sort,—as we

---
* *Ante*, p. 17.
† *Carnatic Papers*, 1861, p. 105.
‡ *Ante*, p. 17.
§ *Carnatic Papers*, 1861, p. 105.
‖ *Ibid.*, 1860, p. 12.

now know from his Despatches, published in 1836;—and that is the sole excuse for Lord Harris's gross inaccuracy. Secure beforehand of the support of Lord Dalhousie, then all powerful with the Home Government, in abolishing what both of them regarded as nothing but an expensive and inconvenient pageant, Lord Harris wrote down with impatient heedlessness his vague recollections of Lord Wellesley's wishes, as described in his Despatches, and passed them off as Lord Wellesley's acts. He introduced Lord Wellesley's abortive plans as if they were finished transactions.

In 1801 Lord Wellesley had two objects in view,—the first was to obtain "the civil and military administration of the Carnatic" from the Nawab with a decent appearance of mutual agreement;—the second was to spread over all the public documents relating to the Nawab's installation a colouring of free gift on the part of the British Government, rather than that of succession by hereditary right. In the first object he succeeded; in the second he completely failed.

Lord Wellesley objected to the original Preamble of the Treaty as concluded by the Governor of Madras, in which it was stated that "the right of Prince Azeem-ood-Dowlah founded upon the hereditary right of his father, the Nawab Ameer-ool-Omrah Bahadoor," had been "*acknowledged* by the English East India Company;" and he contrived to have a new Preamble substituted, declaring that the Nawab had been "*established* by the East India Company in the rank, property, and possessions of his ancestors, heretofore Nabobs of the Carnatic;" but beyond this admission by Azeem-ood-Dowlah of his obligations to the British Government for their support, and of their right, in return, to demand new concessions from him, "*to supply the defects of former engagements*," nothing is gained by the alteration. It is a mere distinction between "acknowledge" and "establish." It does not touch, and was not intended to touch the hereditary nature of the dignity, which, indeed, is fully admitted in the reiterated words, "the rank and dignity of his ancestors," and in the words "succession" and "succeeded" in the Preamble and in Article I. "Succession" to one's "ancestors" implies hereditary right, and can bear no other meaning.

Lord Wellesley attached so little importance to the desired alteration, that he expressly cautioned Lord Clive that it should not be proposed to Azeem-ood-Dowlah "*at the hazard of exciting any alarm or jealousy in his Highness's mind,*" or of incurring his "*dissent or displeasure.*"* And in the meantime, anticipating the possibility of Azeem-ood-Dowlah's objections, Lord Wellesley ratified the original Treaty. This does not look as if he regarded the Nawab as an insignificant person, devoid of political rights. The modified Preamble was accepted by the Nawab without discussion.

The alteration suggested and carried out by Lord Wellesley was not aimed at hereditary succession, past or future, but against the inherent right of the Nawab to succeed unconditionally to the throne, at a political crisis, without British sanction and support.

But whatever advantage Lord Wellesley may be supposed to have gained by these modifications of the Treaty, was quite neutralised and nullified by other solemn and authoritative documents, issued or approved by our Government, in which the hereditary rights of Azeem-ood-Dowlah are emphatically asserted. The Declaration circulated to the Governors of Bombay and Ceylon, and to the Residents at the Courts of Hyderabad and Poonah, and the Proclamation issued to the Chieftains and people of the Carnatic, from both of which we have quoted, not only uphold the "hereditary rights" of Azeem-ood-Dowlah, but go into the particulars of his genealogical descent, as if to contrast them with the doubtful pretensions of the unfortunate Prince who had refused to enter into a new Treaty, and who is insultingly described throughout these state-papers as "*the reputed son,*" and "*the supposed son of Omdut-ool-Oomra.*"†

When the Treaty of 1801 had been concluded, the Nawab, in accordance with the terms of Article XII, issued a circular order "to all his civil and military officers"

* *Carnatic Papers*, 1861, pp. 109, 110.
† *Ibid.*, 1861, p. 107; *Asiatic Annual Register*, 1802, pp. 127 to 133.

to deliver up all the districts, forts, and treasuries to the persons appointed by the Company " to manage" them. The order was drafted by the Governor of Madras himself, translated into Persian, and then submitted to the Nawab Azeem-ood-Dowlah for his seal and signature. This order commenced as follows :—

" Whereas the musnud of the Carnatic Soobadary was vacant, and I the Nawab Wallajah Azeem-ood-Dowlah have *by the grace of God taken possession of the said musnud, in pursuance of the lineal right and title,* as well as with the acknowledgment of the British Company, it is therefore directed that you do immediately on receiving this order deliver without any resistance or excuse the Talooks, etc., under your control into the charge of the officers of the British Company, *who have been appointed with my approval."*

Immediately after his installation, Azeem-ood-Dowlah addressed letters to the King of England, the Prince of Wales, the King of Delhi, the Nizam and the Peishwa, which were perused and approved by Lord Clive, in which he informed them that he had succeeded to the musnud *" by virtue of his right of inheritance."**

On the 3rd of August 1801 the Government of Madras addressed a despatch to the Secret Committee of the Court of Directors, in which occurs the following passage :—

" 'The rights of Omdut-ul-Omrah founded on the Treaty of 1792 having been vitiated by that Prince's violation of the alliance and of the stipulations of that instrument, *the hereditary claims of the House of Mahomed Ally descended to the second branch of the family represented by the Prince Azeem-ood-Dowlah, the son of Ameer-ul-Omrah, who was the second son of the Nabob Mahomed Ally."*†

Lord Harris boldly asserts in his Minute that " Azeem-ood-Dowlah was positively and openly declared to have no hereditary claims."

We have now adduced a sufficiency of positive and open declarations to the contrary effect, and may now challenge his Lordship to point out where those declarations to which he alludes are to be found. They are not to be found; there are no such declarations. And as to Lord Welles-

---

* *Carnatic Papers,* 1861, pp. 113, 115.
† *Ibid.,* 1861, p. 108.

ley's secret and confidential objections to some points in the phraseology employed by Lord Clive, and his opinions as to the penalties that *might* have been inflicted on the Wallajah family, if the British Government had not preferred to act with "magnanimity and generosity," they are nothing to us except as matters of historical or biographical interest. In these days we, and especially the representative of the other contracting party, the rightful Nawab of the Carnatic, have to do only with the Treaty, and the other authoritative documents, such as the Declaration and Proclamation, which were promulgated by our Government to explain the provisions of the Treaty and assist in their execution.

Those who deny the rights of Prince Azeem Jah are by no means consistent or coherent, or, I must be allowed to say, quite ingenuous and straightforward in their arguments. Although they repeatedly say that the case must be decided by the Treaty of 1801, they overlook its main provisions, and are obliged to wander out of them to find the unwarrantable terms of degradation that they think will suit their purpose. Thus Sir Charles Wood, as we have seen, says that "in 1801 the Nawab was reduced to the rank of a pensioner at Madras."* Now even if the Treaty of 1801 were a personal Treaty, which it is not, it would not have "reduced the Nawab to the rank of a pensioner." The "rank and dignity of his ancestors," secured to him by that Treaty, and to his heirs and successors by the old Treaties therein renewed and confirmed,† was not that of a pensioner, but that of hereditary Sovereign of the Carnatic. An "Ally," as he is many times called in the Treaty,‡ could not have been reduced to the rank of a pensioner. "An Independent Prince"§ cannot have been reduced to the rank of a pensioner. The "Sovereign of the Carnatic" and "Superior Lord" of the feudatory Chieftains,"|| among whom were Princes of exalted rank and ancient lineage such as the Rajahs of Travancore and Tanjore, could not have been "reduced

* *Ante*, p. 1.   † *Ante*, pp. 10, 11.
‡ *Ante*, p. 11.   § *Ante*, p. 5.
|| *Ante*, pp. 5, 6.

to the rank of a pensioner." Yet we have seen that the Nawab Azeem-ood-Dowlah was fully recognised in all these capacities.

The advocates of the rapacious policy, however, can shift their ground from one incoherent and inconsistent position to another. If pressed very closely, they may admit that Azeem-ood-Dowlah, with whom the Treaty was concluded, was a Sovereign and not a pensioner, but assert that the Sovereignty ceased at his death, and that his son and grandson were mere pensioners.

Lord Harris writes as follows :—

"The Treaty of 1801 is made with him alone; no mention is made of successors. On his death in 1819 the Government of Madras thought a fresh Treaty was necessary."*

Now this is the truth,—so far,—but it is not the whole truth. The Madras Government did, indeed, suggest in 1819, that a fresh Treaty should be made with Azeem-ood-Dowlah's eldest son, Azum Jah, expressly on account of the succession having been left in an open and doubtful state under the Treaty of 1801, but Lord Harris might have told us a little more. He does not tell us that the Madras Government on that occasion, in their despatch of the 2nd of October, 1819, gave it as their opinion that "the Treaty concluded with the late Nabob on the 31st July, 1801, *had guaranteed the succession to the musnud to his family in the direct and legitimate line of descent;*"† and that the Supreme Government expressed no disagreement with that opinion. The Madras Government simply thought it advisable, " now that the Nawab Azum Jah had virtually become a party" to the Treaty, that he should be called upon "to execute some formal instrument" recognising its conditions. The Governor-General, the Marquis of Hastings, was of opinion that no such new instrument was required, as he considered "his Highness to be *ipso facto* a party to the Treaty concluded with his father in 1801."‡

Lord Dalhousie's comment upon this first succession

---

* *Carnatic Papers*, 1860, p. 12.
† *Ibid.*, p. 35.   ‡ *Ibid.*, pp. 35 and 40.

after the new settlement appears to me to be singularly disingenuous. He says:—

"Upon the death of Azeem-ood-Dowlah the Treaty of 1801 was not renewed. It has never since been renewed. *The Government of India on a former occasion expressly declined to renew it.* The Treaty of 1801, therefore, has had no existence, and its provisions have had no binding force since the death of the Nawab Azeem-ood-Dowlah, with whom it was concluded, and to whom alone it was applicable."*

Now it certainly is true that the Treaty of 1801 has never been renewed; it is true that the Government of India declined to renew it, but not, as Lord Dalhousie insinuates, because they looked on it as void and did not wish it to be made valid, but because they looked on it as still valid; not because, as Lord Dalhousie asserts, "it was applicable to the Nawab Azeem-ood-Dowlah alone," but because his son and successor was "*ipso facto,*" (by the fact of his succession,) "*a party to it;*" not because a renewal was considered impolitic, but because it was considered superfluous. Both in the questions asked by the Government of Madras, and in the answers given by the Supreme Government, the supposed new instrument was discussed as a matter of form only, and not as a matter of policy. The question of the continuance or cessation of the Nawab's dignity was never raised at all.

Lord Dalhousie says "the Treaty of 1801 *has had no existence, and its provisions have had no binding force,* since the death of the Nawab Azeem-ood-Dowlah." Let us see whether this is true or not. Lord Hastings in 1819, at the death of Azeem-ood-Dowlah, said that his son and successor was "*ipso facto* a party" to the Treaty. The Supreme Government said that "their resolution to continue to the Nawab the dignities and benefits of his deceased father under the provisions *of the existing Treaty,* combined with the cheerful acceptance of the same at their hands, would constitute *a confirmation of the existing Treaty,* preferable, considering the relative situation of the parties, to the formal conclusion of precise stipulations."†

* *Carnatic Papers,* 1860, p. 48.
† *Ibid.,* p. 35.

Lord Dalhousie says that the Treaty, spoken of by Lord Hastings in 1819, after the death of Azeem-ood-Dowlah, as "*the existing Treaty*," "*had no existence*" after the death of Azeem-ood-Dowlah. Lord Dalhousie says that the "provisions" of that Treaty, which according to Lord Hastings underwent "confirmation" after the death of Azeem-ood-Dowlah, "have had no binding force since the death of Azeem-ood-Dowlah." Hardly another word is necessary to show that Lord Dalhousie was quite wrong. An existing Treaty certainly has existence. Provisions that are confirmed certainly continue to have binding force.

The existing Treaty having been thus recognised and confirmed at the death of Azeem-ood-Dowlah, his eldest son, Azum Jah, was enthroned, and was congratulated by the Governor of Madras on "ascending the Musnud in the direct line of hereditary succession to his late father of blessed memory."* The Governor concluded his address with these words :—

"Under the sanction of the Most Noble the Governor-General, and *your acknowledgment of the validity of the Treaty, its stipulations are now declared to be equally binding upon your Highness, as they were upon the late Nawab and the British Government.*"†

On the death of Azeem-ood-Dowlah in 1819, the Governor of Madras, with the full knowledge and approval of the Supreme Government, publicly announces "the validity of the Treaty," and declares its stipulations to be "*binding*" upon both parties, upon the Nawab and the British Government. In 1855 Lord Dalhousie, wishing to get rid of the Treaty, boldly declares that "it has had no existence," and that "its provisions have had *no binding force* since the death of the Nawab Azeem-ood-Dowlah."

Upon such manifest contradictions of the truth, and defiance of recorded facts, is built the denial of Prince Azeem Jah's rights.

In the reign of the Nawab Azum Jah, elder brother of

---

* *Carnatic Papers*, 1860, p. 129.
† *Ibid.*, 1861, p. 129.

Prince Azeem Jah, Sir Thomas Munro, then Governor of Madras, thus referred to the Treaty of 1801 :—

" By this the Nawab *does not relinquish his Sovereignty*.

" The fifth part of the revenue is his claim *as Sovereign of the whole Carnatic.*

" He is still *Prince of the Carnatic, and he is a party to the Treaty by which one-fifth part of the revenue is secured to him.*

" The present assumption of the country is permanent, *but the relative situations of the Company, and the Nawab, are the same as in former cases of assumption. The Nawab is still Prince of the Carnatic,* and receives in that capacity one-fifth of the net revenue."*

In speaking of "*former cases of assumption,*"—when under the old Treaties the Company assumed the administration of the Carnatic during war,—Sir Thomas Munro declares that the "relative situations" of the Company and the son of Azeem-ood-Dowlah, are the same as in the time of the Nawab's predecessors, before the Treaty of 1801 was concluded.

It is perfectly clear, therefore, that the son of the Nawab with whom the Treaty of 1801 was concluded, was not "reduced to the rank of a pensioner," and that during his life-time the Carnatic territories were not annexed.

We now come to the late Nawab, Gholam Mahomed Ghous Khan, only son of Azum Jah. His father died in 1825, and he was proclaimed "successor to the rank and title of Nawab Soubadar of the Carnatic," his uncle, Prince Azeem Jah, being appointed Regent during his nephew's minority. There was certainly no doubt or hesitation at that time as to the hereditary nature of the Nawab's dignity.

The able and eminent lawyer, Mr. Thomas Sydney Smyth, who was Advocate-General at Madras when the late Nawab died, in one of his official letters to Government, incidentally—perhaps accidentally—places in its true light the striking testimony to the Nawab's hereditary Sovereignty afforded by the circumstances attending his accession. The letter in question, (printed at the Government Press of Madras) is dated May 30th, 1859, and was intended to fix the liability for certain debts incurred

* *Gleig's Life of Sir Thomas Munro,* vol. ii, p. 356.

during the late Nawab's minority upon Prince Azeem Jah. The italics are in the original.

"When the late Nabob's father died, the Government, in 1825, '*recognised*' the infant Nabob as his lawful successor; but it *appointed*, of its own authority, (by an official letter and Proclamation in the Gazette) the Prince to conduct the affairs of the Circar during the minority, as Naib-i-Mooktar."

The distinction here drawn between the *recognition* of a "*lawful successor*," and the *appointment*, "by its own authority," of a Guardian by our Government, is of vital importance, and negatives at once the notion of the late Nawab having been "reduced to the rank of a pensioner," or of his having succeeded to the musnud by the "grace and favour" of the other contracting party to the Treaty. He was, as the learned Advocate-General justly observed, "the lawful successor" to his father.

From the same collection of documents we find that the British Government designated the late Nawab, immediately after his accession, as their "Ally." In a Minute by the Governor of Madras, Sir Thomas Munro, dated the 3rd of February, 1826, the following sentence occurs:—

"It may be expected that the Court of Directors will not disapprove of such an advance of money as may be requisite to liberate their ancient Ally, the Nabob of the Carnatic, from all pecuniary embarrassment."

We have already adduced the payment to the Nawab Azeem-ood-Dowlah of the annual tribute due from his feudatory, the Rajah of Travancore, as sufficient evidence that the Sovereignty of the Carnatic was not resigned by the Nawab Azeem-ood-Dowlah in the Treaty of 1801. This feudal supremacy was maintained during the reign of his son and successor, and was upheld to the day of his grandson, the late Nawab's decease, and even beyond it! The Travancore Peishcush always continued to be paid into the Nawab's treasury; but since the late Nawab's death, it has been transferred to the Madras Government, and appears among the receipts of 1861-62 with the following extraordinary entry:—"Rajah of Travancore, *on account of the late Nabob of the Carnatic*,—13,320 Rupees."*

---

* *Madras Administration Report*, 1861-2, para. 604, p. 106.

We know by the terms already quoted from the official records of the Madras Government, that this tribute was paid to the Nawab as "Sovereign of the Carnatic."*

There is ample evidence also that the Treaty of 1801 was acknowledged to be in full force during the reign of the late Nawab, Mahomed Ghous Khan. For example, the Madras Government, "after quoting the fifth Article of the Treaty, remarked in Extract from the Minutes of Consultation, dated 7th December 1847, that these ladies having long enjoyed the stipends assigned to them, the character and good faith of the British Government were concerned, and that His Highness was *bound by the Treaty* to support them."† Here the Nawab is declared in the year 1847 to be "bound by the Treaty," which Lord Dalhousie asserted to have had "no binding force," and "no existence," since the year 1819.

The Sovereignty of the Nawab was thus maintained without dispute or question during the reign of Prince Azeem Jah's nephew, and the Treaty of 1801 was declared to be in force. It is evident, therefore, that the late Nawab was not "reduced to the rank of a pensioner at Madras," and no annexation of the Carnatic territories had taken place up to the date of his death, the 7th of October, 1855.

So far as the claims of Prince Azeem Jah are concerned, there can be no objection to our statesmen declaring that his father, brother and nephew were merely "nominal" or "titular" Sovereigns, and that all practical and substantial power was lodged in the hands of the East India Company. That is perfectly true. In claiming the hereditary Sovereignty of the Carnatic, secured by a series of uncancelled treaties—including the Treaty of Paris—to the Wallajah family, Prince Azeem Jah claims no regal authority to interfere with or influence the legislative or executive action of our Government.

If our Government chooses to fall foul of its own work

---

* *Ante*, p. 5.
† Papers relating to Carnatic Stipendiaries, Madras, 1858, p. 327. There are many similar references to the Treaty to be found in the Proceedings of the Madras Government.

and to pour contempt upon its Ally by calling him "a pageant" or "a puppet," it will not help us in the least towards obtaining the Sovereignty of the Carnatic, of which we have never pretended to divest him, and of which he has never divested himself.

Our power over the revenues and resources of the Carnatic has been practical and substantial enough for the last sixty-seven years, but only by virtue of the Treaty of 1801. We have never conquered an acre of it. Not an acre of it has ever passed to the British Government in sovereignty, by cession, by escheat or lapse, by Imperial Act or popular vote, by any process known to the old Law of Nations, or to modern revolutionary doctrine. Our contumacious possession of the Carnatic, while we refuse the royal dignity and the stipulated share of the revenue to the Sovereign, our Ally, would stand the test of neither a Congress nor a *plébiscite*.

We have nothing to show for it but the Nawab's grant of the Chingleput Jaghire,* and the Treaty of 1801. The grantor of a Jaghire resigns no Sovereignty; he expressly asserts it; the grantee admits it. Under the Treaty of 1801 the Nawab remained the Sovereign, the Company became the Administrator and Trustee of his dominions. But the Treaty that gave over to the Company all practical and substantial power, that invested it with "the civil and military administration" "for ever," contained also some practical and substantial stipulations in favour of the Nawab. He was "established in the rank, property and possessions of his ancestors, with the dignities dependent thereon," and a fifth share of the revenues, after certain deductions, was allotted for his support, to "be at his free disposal, consistently with the principles of the alliance."†

If, therefore, the practical and substantial provisions in favour of the Nawab are not observed by the other contracting party, the British Government, the Treaty is violated, and their right to "the civil and military administration" of the Carnatic, their "full and exclusive right to

---

* *Collection of Treaties*, vol. v, p. 196.
† *Article* v,—*Collection of Treaties*, vol. v, p. 250.

the revenues thereof, (with the exception of the portion reserved for the Nawab,)"* having never rested upon anything but the Treaty, falls to the ground. Henceforward our footing in the Carnatic, until rectified by some act of state, or some new convention, is utterly untenable and indefinable under the Law of Nations. We occupy a perfectly lawless position. Our Government has neither a title to the territory to set before other States and Sovereigns, nor a claim to allegiance and obedience to set before the inhabitants of the Carnatic.

Sir Charles Wood said we might " dismiss all question of the annexation of territory,"—in other words, that the Carnatic territories were not annexed *at the death* of the late Nawab. I have shown that they were not annexed *before his death*. I believe that Sir Charles Wood was quite right, and that no annexation has been effected. The British Government since 1855, not only has had no valid title to the Carnatic territories, but has gone through no process, forcible or diplomatic, to set up a colourable title. The Treaty is violated; and we are now wrongfully administering those territories, without any authority that will bear examination or that is capable of public avowal.

The right of conquest gives a good title, when confirmed by time and popular approval. By such a title we hold Pegu, the King of Burmah having always refused to sign any treaty for the cession of that Province. No one would question our title to the Punjaub, for though the process for deposing our infant Ward, was more stealthy than straightforward until all resistance was overcome,† still there were military operations deserving the name of war; we called it a conquest, and no one contradicted us; we took an instrument resigning the Sovereignty from the young Prince and the leading Chieftains ;‡ and we issued a Proclamation declaring the country annexed to the British dominions.

---

* Articles iv and v, *Collection of Treaties*, vol. v, p. 250.

† *Retrospects and Prospects of Indian Policy*, Chapter on the Punjaub, especially pp. 142 to 158.

‡ *Collection of Treaties*, Calcutta, vol. ii, p. 271.

But we have no right of conquest in the Carnatic. We have no right over those territories except that of "civil and military administration" acquired by the Treaty of 1801, subject to certain conditions with which we have wrongfully dispensed. We have no act or instrument to show; we have issued no Proclamation. It would be impossible for anyone to draw up a Proclamation declaring the Sovereignty of the Carnatic to have passed from the Nawab to the British Government, without there being a manifest falsehood on the face of it.

Nor has our position improved in the least during the few years that have elapsed since the death of Prince Azeem Jah's nephew, the Nawab Mahomed Ghous Khan. We have certainly acquired no right by Usucaption or Prescription, for, as we have just seen, throughout the late Nawab's reign the existence of his Sovereignty and alliance with us, the maintenance of the Treaty of 1801, and our administrative trust under it, were never disputed,* and since his decease the lawful heir and successor has kept up a continuous claim. Prescription is entirely on the side of the Wallajah family.†

There can be no doubt about our material power to retain possession of all the revenues of the Carnatic, and to continue exercising the " civil and military administration" of those Provinces, while rejecting the claims of Prince Azeem Jah, or any descendant of his, the representative for the time being of the line of hereditary Sovereigns, the other contracting party to the Treaty of 1801. And yet, to those who can look a little beyond the ways and means of the day, it might seem that, even to a great military Empire, a good title for every territorial possession is of some value,—the more valuable in the case of far distant possessions, where the will of an alien population has not been, and cannot be consulted.

The temptation to do us an injury, to shake our influence, or to meet some remonstrance of ours with a telling retort, might induce a rival Power to challenge some of

---

* *Ante*, pp. 30, 31.

† See *Grotius, Droit de la Guerre et de la Paix*, liv. ii, chap. iv, Amsterdam, 1724.

our Indian titles. At any time it would have an unsettling effect, if European diplomacy were to claim the right of inquiry, or to display the least interest in the origin and extent of our hitherto unquestioned supremacy and vast direct possessions. At a critical time, in the midst of war, rebellion or general excitement, any well-founded remonstrance, taunt or imputation might be very embarrassing, if not injurious. Let us be able to answer a summons to the bar of European opinion by a plain and candid statement of our rights and titles. Above all, when such a summons shall be issued,—and it may be nearer than we suppose,—let it meet with no guilty response in our national conscience, with no indignant welcome in the hearts of the Indian people. Let right be done!

With reference to the alleged treachery and perfidy of the Nawab Mahomed Ali Wallajah and his son Omdutool-Oomra, which are said to have compelled and justified the deposition of the family from power, that account, as I have already said, was closed by the Treaty of 1801. Whatever may have been the justice of that transaction, so long as its provisions are kept in force, and its stipulations observed on both sides, neither party has any right to stir up its grounds once more. That question is not reopened by Prince Azeem Jah, but by those who impugn his claim. And before proceeding farther, we must here notice one strange mistake into which several Members of Parliament fell in the debates on this subject. For example, on the 14th of March, 1865, Sir Robert Collier, then Solicitor-General, tried to limit the range of discussion by the following extraordinary statement:—

"It was only by the Treaty of 1801 that the present claimant must stand, for if the former Treaties were in force he would not be the right heir, and instead of sitting upon the throne he would probably have found himself in a dungeon."*

* *Hansard*, vol. clxxvii, p. 1700. Exactly the same thing had been previously said by Mr. Grenfell in the debate of 13th July, 1864.—*Hansard*, vol. clxxv, p. 1655.

The present claimant is perfectly willing to stand by the Treaty of 1801: he demands nothing more than the dignities and revenues guaranteed to his family by that instrument. The former Treaties have been proved to be still in force, so far as they are not modified by the Treaty of 1801, with which they are inseparably bound up, in which they are categorically recited, renewed and confirmed.* The present claimant has no reason to shun the former Treaties. If the Treaty of 1801 had never been made, he would still be the lineal heir, and there would be no better claimant in existence to put him into the supposed dungeon. When Ali Hoossain, " the reputed son" of Omdut-ool-Oomra, who refused to make the new Treaty, died without issue in 1802, the present claimant's father, the Nawab Azeem-ood-Dowlah, became the undisputed representative, both in the male and female lines, of the first Nawab.

The opponents of Prince Azeem Jah's rights try to pin him down to the Treaty of 1801,—to which he does not object,—while they wander away from it themselves. They fetter him with its restrictions, to which he submits,—as did his father, brother and nephew,—while they refuse him its privileges. They will not permit the oppressive proceedings of 1801 to rest in peace. Frivolous charges of secret conspiracy having been used as a pretext for extorting the Treaty of 1801, they bring them forward again to destroy the residue of advantages reserved to the Wallajah family by that extorted Treaty. The employment of those wretched calumnies in 1801 was bad enough; the attempt to make them do double duty after the lapse of more than half a century is still worse. Having been freely paraded by Lords Harris and Dalhousie in 1855, to cast obloquy and contempt on the Wallajah family as detected conspirators, and to strengthen the probability and propriety of their having been left dependent on the " grace and favour" of the British Government, they make their appearance again when redress or inquiry is demanded in the House of Commons. Thus in the debate of the 13th of June, 1864, on Mr. Smollett's motion for a Select

* *Ante*, pp. 10, 11.

Committee, Sir James Fergusson, Member for Ayrshire, made the following assertion :—

"It was proved that in defiance of the Treaty of 1792 the Nawab of the Carnatic had been in constant communication with Tippoo Sultan, giving him secret information."*

And on the same occasion the Right Hon. Robert Lowe repeated the same charges.

"When we took Seringapatam we discovered that a correspondence of a highly treasonable nature had been carried on in cypher, which proved that the Nawab was one of the allies of Tippoo Sultan. Unfortunately for the Nawab the key to the cypher was also found, so that the meaning of the correspondence became known."†

Premising what will in due course be shown with perfect clearness, that no secret or treasonable correspondence between the Nawabs and Tippoo Sultan was ever discovered at all, it will be advisable, before touching on these trumped up charges, to show what were the relations existing between the Nawabs of the Carnatic and the East India Company, and what were the points in dispute between them in the year 1801.

Our previous dealings with the Nawabs of the Carnatic have been wonderfully misrepresented in the official despatches and, as a natural consequence, in Parliamentary speeches. Lord Harris, for instance, whose position as Governor of Madras gave him perfect command of every source of information, displays the most incredible ignorance, not only of the past history of the Wallajah family, and of the ties connecting them with our Government, but even of notorious facts relating to them that existed, or were passing under his own nose. From the origin of the first Nawab's power in the Carnatic down to the actual number of Prince Azeem Jah's sons,‡ his Lordship's Minute positively bristles with blunders.

As to the origin of the Nawabs' Sovereignty, Lord Harris contradicts himself in the most flagrant manner. He first

---

* *Hansard*, vol. clxxv, p. 1659. † *Ibid.*, p. 1669.

‡ He says in para. 60 of his Minute, (*Carnatic Papers*, 1860, p. 14), that "Prince Azeem Jah has no legitimate sons." He has four,—(1.) Zaheer-ood-Dowla Mahomed Badee Oollah Khan; (2.) Intizam-ool-Moolk Ahmed-oollah Khan : (3.) Oomdut-ood-Dowlah Noor-oolla Khan; and (4.) Mowzaz-ood-Dowla Mahee-ood-deen Yar Khan.

throws doubt on their ever having been Sovereigns at all, notwithstanding the innumerable documents and despatches in the records of his own Government,—some of which we have quoted,*—in which each successive Nawab is declared to be "an independent Prince," and "Sovereign of the Carnatic."

" The hereditary right to the Carnatic, the royal title and privileges, were assumed and certainly allowed by us; but I imagine on no authority which could be considered legal for a Mussulman subject of the Mogul.

" What power, what influence may have been possessed, has now passed away, and cannot be recalled. They were acquired by the prestige of Mussulman conquest; they have vanished with the decadence of its power."†

In a postscript to his Minute, while persisting that all this is "substantially correct," he admits having ascertained from the records of Government that in 1765 "the appointment of Mahomed Ali to the Sovereignty of the Carnatic was confirmed by a firman from the Mogul Emperor of Delhi."‡ If we add to this our own acknowledgment and that of the Nizam in the Treaty of 1768,§ and the guaranty of Mahomed Ali in Article XI of the Treaty of Paris in 1763 as " the legitimate Nawab of the Carnatic,"‖ what better or more " legal authority" can Lord Harris have expected to find?

But Lord Harris says, " the power and influence" of the Nawabs " were acquired by the prestige of Mussulman conquest; they have vanished with the decadence of its power." This opinion is not exactly consistent with that given in the postscript, that " the elevation of this family was entirely and solely owing to the assistance they received from the British power."¶

Contradictory, however, as they are, it is difficult to

---

* *Ante*, pp. 4 to 6, and 23 to 31.
† *Carnatic Papers*, 1860, p. 14.
‡ *Ibid.*, p. 36.
§ *Collection of Treaties*, vol. 5, p. 21.
‖ " Et afin de conserver la Paix future sur la Côte de *Coromandel* et d'*Orixa*, les Anglois et les François réconnoitront *Mahomet Ally Khan* pour Légitime Nabob du Carnate." *Martens' Recueil*, tome i, p. 113.
¶ *Carnatic Papers*, 1860, p. 37.

say which of these two statements is the more inaccurate. Most certainly "the power and influence" of the Wallajah family were not acquired by "the prestige of Mussulman conquest." When Anwar-ood-deen, the first Nawab of the family, was raised to the Deputy Governorship of the Carnatic in time of profound peace by his immediate Suzerain the Nizam, Mussulman conquest had ceased entirely. Mussulman ascendancy was *then* in "its decadence."

It would be much more true to say that "the power and influence of the Nawabs were acquired"—certainly were established,—" by the prestige" of British friendship and British good faith, and "vanished with the decadence" of the same. Here is an extract from a Minute by the President of Fort St. George in Council, dated 4th February, 1779 :—" All attention and support is certainly due to the Nabob as our old and faithful Ally, connected with us by every tie, and demanding from us every indulgence ;" and the Minute concludes with these memorable words—" who, *with his family*, it is to be wished, *may long remain instances of our national faith.*"* His family remains ; but of which of our national characteristics its treatment is to afford an instance, is, I trust, still undecided.

The firm establishment of the Nawab's Sovereignty was certainly due in a great measure to British friendship and good faith ; but Lord Harris is quite wrong when he says that "the elevation of this family was entirely and solely owing to the assistance they received from the British power."†

Mr. Lowe, in his speech of the 13th of June, 1864, misled probably by Lord Harris, and surpassing him in error by venturing on circumstantiality, said :—

"The first of the Nawabs of the Carnatic "(meaning, I suppose, the first of this family) " owed his elevation to the power of England, and as a reward for the assistance he had given her in the struggle between Lawrence and Dupleix."‡

* *Carnatic Papers*, 1861, p. 51.
† *Ante*, p. 38.
‡ *Hansard*, vol. clxxv, p. 1667.

Let us compare these very inaccurate statements with the historical facts. When Anwar-ood-deen Khan, the founder of the Wallajah family, having previously been Nawab of Chicacole, was elevated to the dignity of Nawab of the Carnatic, the British authorities in India had no voice in the matter. Anwar-ood-deen Khan became Nawab in 1744, on the death of the infant Mohammed Saeed, the fourth of a family who had filled the musnud of the Carnatic in hereditary succession, and who during the convulsions of the Mogul Empire had withheld the payment of tribute, and assumed a position of semi-independence. The office of Nawab was originally held by commission from the Emperor at Delhi, but in the event of any delay in filling up a vacancy, the Nizam of the Deccan claimed the right of nomination. During the decay of the Empire, however, the Imperial Commission had come to be regarded merely as an honourable form of confirmation to be obtained at any convenient opportunity; and the right of appointment was tacitly, if not openly contested between the Nawab and the Nizam,— the latter claiming it as his prerogative, the former striving to render it hereditary in his family.*

The British Governors of Madras had always paid rent for the town of Madras and its dependencies, and had sent periodical presents to all Anwar-ood-deen's predecessors, and although exercising full jurisdiction within the limits of the settlement, never failed to recognise "the Country Government," and to show great deference to the Nawab. On each succession the Government of Madras always sought from the Nawab a renewal of its privileges and immunities.

The following extracts from the official records now at Madras will prove how utterly erroneous is Lord Harris's assertion that "the elevation of the family was entirely and solely owing to the assistance they received from the British power."†

---

* *Beveridge's Comprehensive History of India*, (Blackie, 1866) vol. i, p. 430. *Orme's History*, 1780, vol. i, p. 54.

† *Ante*, p. 38.

"Monday, 2nd April, 1744. The President acquaints the Board that agreeable to the advices from the country he communicated to us on the 5th instant, he is since informed that the Nizam-ool-Moolk being returned to a place in the province called Gundecotta, about eight days' journey distant from Arcot, has fixed the appointments to the several Nabobships of Cundanore, Golconda, Corrapa, and Arcot, the last of which he had bestowed on Khoja Abdulla Khan. But he dying the night he received his commission, the Nizam had conferred it on Anwar-ood-deen Khan, another of his officers and late Nabob of Chicacolo, a person generally well esteemed, and said to be very agreeable to the people."

"Monday, 23rd, April, 1744. The President observes to the Board that Anwar-ood-deen Khan being now fixed in the Government, we must think of preparing a present for him and the other officers as usual."*

The following extracts from the same interesting work we have just quoted, will show that in the earlier stages of our connection with this family, we owed much more to the Nawabs than they owed to us. In the very year of Anwar-ood-deen's accession, war had broken out between Great Britain and France. The French attained to a temporary ascendancy on the Eastern Coast of India; Madras was taken in September 1746; and the British Governor was reduced to great straits in Fort St. David at Cuddalore. Here is an extract of a despatch from Governor Hinde to the Court of Directors, dated the 10th of January, 1747:

"The only alteration in our favour since we wrote you last is, that we have prevailed with the Country Government to declare in our favour; and in consequence of it the Nabob sent his son Mahomed Ali Khan" (afterwards the Nawab Wallajah) "with about 2000 Horse to our assistance the beginning of last month. Notwithstanding which, the French thought proper the 8th ultimo to come against us with their whole force from Pondicherry; when we made the best defence we were able; and, notwithstanding they got so far as the Garden House, we had the good fortune on the 9th to drive them out and compel them to a very precipitate retreat.

"The Nabob was so well disposed towards us, but as yet we have not had a line or any assistance from Bengal since Madras

* *Madras in the Olden Time*, compiled from the Official Records, by J. Talboys Wheeler, (now Assistant Secretary to the Government of India in the Foreign Department,) Madras, 1861, vol. iii, p. 398.

was taken,—now four months. The Nabob's oldest son, Mafooz Khan, is now joined his brother, and the expense of the camp amounts to upwards of 6000 rupees per day; and they with reason grow extremely impatient, and we fear will quit our interest, if some ships do not appear soon to assist us."*

"Hitherto we have been but at a small expense, our presents to the Country Government not exceeding above 3000 pagodas" (£10,500), "a trifle not worth mentioning in proportion to the expense they are at, and the disquiet it hath given our enemies, who are trying all possible methods to make up affairs with them. We have in general terms promised in your Honours' name that we will not be ungrateful for any favour the Nabob inclines to show us."†

The following extract is taken from a letter to the Court of Directors, dated the 2nd of May, 1747, by Charles Floyer, Deputy-Governor in the room of Mr. Hinde, who had lately died :—

"The presents that we made them, whilst the Nabob's two armies were encamped without our bounds, for near three months, at an expense of upwards 6000 rupees a day in our defence, did not amount to above 40,000 rupees, which in comparison to the services they were of in defeating the French in their attempt upon this place on the 9th December, we are of opinion you will allow to be very inconsiderable."‡

So far it does not seem as if "the elevation of the family" were—as Lord Harris would persuade us,—"entirely and solely owing to the assistance they received from the British power". So far, they do not seem to have had much reason to be grateful to us.

The next noticeable incident in our friendly relations with "the Country Government", is that the aged Nawab Anwar-ood-deen was killed at the battle of Amboor, on the 3rd of August, 1749, fought against the French and Chunda Sahib, connected by marriage with the family previously occupying the musnud, who had been set up by Dupleix, the Governor of Pondicherry, as a pretender to the Nawabship, with a view to the destruction of British influence. So far, the Wallajah family does not seem to have owed us much gratitude.

From that time down to 1763, when Mahomed Ali Khan was recognised by the Treaty of Paris as "legitimate Na-

* *Madras in the Olden Time*, vol. iii, p. 398.
† *Ibid.*, p. 399.   ‡ *Ibid.*, p. 403.

wab of the Carnatic", the obligations of the Nawab and the Company were, to say the least, reciprocal, and tolerably equal. If our Government provided the handful of gallant officers and stalwart British soldiers who alone could lead and discipline the Native troops, and withstand the French Infantry; if we found the more serviceable Artillery, the best munitions and materials of war, the Nawab for his part secured all the necessary supplies, found all the Cavalry, and—which was of still more importance,—nearly all the money.

Besides this, it must be remembered that the sole cause of all Mahomed Ali's difficulties, the sole reason of his requiring our assistance almost as much as we required his, was our quarrel with the French. The French had no quarrel with his father or with him, except on our account. There was nobody to dispute his hereditary claim, and no probability of any one doing so; until the French, finding him firmly opposed to their repeated overtures, procured the release of Chunda Sahib from captivity at Sattara, and espoused his cause, with the sole object of annoying the British Government. Mahomed Ali could have held his own quite well without our help, if he had not been entangled in our war with France. Without his assistance we must have been destroyed.

The services rendered by the Nawab Wallajah are acknowledged in the following terms by the Court of Directors in a letter to His Highness dated the 1st of June 1764:—

"The assurances Mr. Pigot, our late Governor of Madras, has given us of your continued attachment to the Company, and the strong proofs you have yourself produced of your generous attention and good will, in taking on yourself the whole charges of the sieges of Madras and Pondicherry, and in the grants you have lately made to the Company of lands in the vicinity of Madras, are pleasing and acceptable to us in the highest degree. We are at a loss how to express our acknowledgments otherwise than by the strongest assurance of our firm intention to prove to you at once the sincerity of our past and the warmth of our present friendship, by supporting you in the most effectual manner in your government, and by endeavouring as much as in us lies *to perpetuate the succession thereof in the direct line of your family.*"*

* *Carnatic Papers*, 1861, p. 46.

Prince Azeem Jah is a direct lineal descendant in the male line of the Nawab Wallajah. This promise was renewed by an autograph letter from His Majesty George III to the Nawab Wallajah, dated the 19th March, 1771, in the following terms :—

"We received from the hands of our East India Company, in July last, your letter, accompanied with your different presents. We shall look upon the picture of yourself and your children with pleasure, as it will put us continually in mind of that affection which you have always shown towards us, and which we have no doubt will be hereditary in your offspring, as we are satisfied that *our friendship and protection to you and your posterity will descend through our successors from generation to generation."*

Sir Thomas Rumbold, Governor of Madras, writing in January 1780, remarks as follows on the advantages derived from the Nawab's friendship :—

"It is unquestionably to this influence that we are indebted for a great part of our prosperity, for our success against the French in India in the last war, and for the decisive stroke made against them so early in the present war, *to which,* as affairs have since turned out, *we owe perhaps our present existence in the East."**

Yet Lord Harris, Governor of Madras in 1855, says that "the elevation of this family was entirely and solely owing to the assistance they received from the British power."†

From 1763 down to 1785, when Preliminary Articles of Agreement were drawn up, converted in 1787 into "a Treaty of perpetual friendship, alliance and security", between the Honourable East India Company and His Highness the Nawab Wallajah, "his heirs and successors",‡ (one of the Treaties recited in the Preamble, "renewed and confirmed" in Article II of the Treaty of 1801,) there was no alteration in their relative situations, though a great alteration had gradually been effected in their relative strength. The only documentary connection consisted of grants of land and revenue from the Nawab as Sovereign of the Carnatic to the Company as Jaghiredar, "in consideration of the many services rendered to his affairs".§

* *Carnatic Papers,* 1861, p. 52.
† *Ante,* p. 38.
‡ *Collection of Treaties,* vol. v, p. 227.
§ *Ibid.,* p. 196.

It was only through "the Country Government" that a hold could be got on the resources of the Carnatic in men or money; and even if the undeviating friendship of the Nawab had afforded any pretext, no scheme of territorial conquest was practicable. By degrees, however, during the wars with Hyder Ali and Tippoo Sultan, the power of the East India Company had increased enormously. Their arms and arts had prospered greatly in Bengal. Oude was a virtual tributary. The Company's trade was rapidly becoming a secondary consideration. Their representatives at the three Presidencies, now openly supported by the Government of Great Britain and the King's troops, no longer sued for mercantile privileges; they contracted military alliances, and though still professing the allegiance of vassals to the Emperor, and preserving certain forms of deference and submission in addressing the Nizam of the Deccan, dealt as an independent Power and on equal terms with all the Princes of India.

About the year 1775 the Nawab maintained an army of about 40,000 men, a great part being troops of good quality. In a letter from the Madras Government dated the 4th of July, 1775, it is stated:—

"The Nawab's second son, Ameer-ool-Oomra,* has seven distinct corps, consisting of Cavalry, light-armed Sepoys, and Artillery; 12 Battalions of Sepoys, with near 1000 Artillery,—all which are far better disciplined than those of any of the Country Powers. Some of his black Cavalry, we are informed, are as well disciplined as any of the English troops; his Artillery attached to them may vie almost with Europeans."†

The number of the Nawab's own troops was from time to time diminished in some proportion to the increased demand of the Company for subsidies to pay their own more efficient forces. There seems to have been a considerable reduction in 1784 by a process of transfer to the service of the Madras Government. On the 27th of May, 1784, the *Calcutta Gazette* informs us, through "private letters from Madras", that

* Father of Azeem-ood-Dowlah, with whom the Treaty of 1801 was made, grandfather of Prince Azeem Jah.
† *Carnatic Papers*, 1861, p. 54.

"The Nabob's troops are taken into the Company's Service. The European officers come in the youngest of their rank."*

In the year 1787, when the Nawab Mahomed Ali Wallajah had been in close alliance with us for upwards of forty years,—the greater part of that time having been passed in constant war with the French, Hyder and Tippoo,—he had granted the Company lands in Jaghire producing about £200,000 a year, and was paying annually about £650,000,—more than half the gross revenue of his remaining dominions,—in subsidy for British troops, and as instalments of his debt to the Honourable Company. He was the great pay-master, and yet, somehow or other, he was always on the wrong side of the account. His difficulties were fearfully aggravated by the unprincipled rapacity of the English officials of all ranks, even the very highest. Some insight into this disgraceful history may be gained from the debate of the 28th of February, 1785, on Mr. Fox's motion for "papers relative to the Nabob of Arcot's private debts to Europeans, charged on the revenues of the Carnatic".† The worst feature in this discreditable affair is that neither the House of Commons nor His Majesty's Government took any adequate steps to stigmatise the delinquents, or to prevent them from gathering the fruits of their iniquitous and fraudulent extortion. The Ministry, secure of a majority against Mr. Fox's motion, and determined to retain the purchased Parliamentary influence of Paul Benfield and his accomplices, would not even attempt a reply to the great speech of Burke on this occasion. The motion for inquiry was resisted without the semblance of discussion. The Board of Control altered the despatches of the Court of Directors in order to secure the interests of the so-called "private creditors" of the Nawab, which the Directors had refused to promote.‡

These humiliating incidents, always distasteful, never

---

* *Selections from the Calcutta Gazettes*, 1784 to 1788, compiled with the sanction of Government by W. S. Seton-Karr, Esq., Calcutta, 1864 (London, Longman and Co.)

† *Hansard's Parliamentary History*, vol. xxv, pp. 163 to 259.

‡ *Mill's History of India* (edited by H. H. Wilson) vol. v, pp. 25 to 40.

fully appreciated or believed, and now almost forgotten in Great Britain, are thoroughly understood and held in vivid recollection at Madras and Hyderabad. There every one capable of having an opinion and taking an interest in political and historical questions,—the great noble and rich banker as well as the petty shopkeeper or the common Sepoy—has heard from his old relations or neighbours, how dearly the good Nawab Wallajah was made to pay for the blessings of British protection; how all the English gentlemen,—from the King on his throne down to the Ensign on guard in Fort St. George,—had to be propitiated with presents, while those in high local authority demanded vast sums, either in ready money or in acknowledgments of fictitious debt, and how, when by his aid British power had been firmly established, all was in vain to save his family from dethronement, pillage and defamation.

There is much less exaggeration here than could be wished. But, however much or little exaggerated these imputations may be, they rest upon a sufficient groundwork of notorious facts to secure them from being shaken by the storm of mere indignant denials with which, on first hearing them, an Englishman ignorant of Indian history,—and there are many such at home and abroad,—would be inclined to meet them. Exaggerated or not, such is the current tradition of Southern India as to our treatment of the Wallajah family in the last century; and short-sighted indeed was the policy—to say nothing of its justice and generosity,—which revived, renewed and confirmed the current tradition in 1855, and has played over again before the people of Southern India the old scenes of dethronement, pillage, and defamation.

The oppressive uncertainty of the pecuniary demands on the Nawab was reduced to an endurable regularity by the engagements of 1785 and 1787, considerably mitigated by Lord Cornwallis's Treaty of 1792, and still more by the stringent measures for checking official plunder enforced by that upright ruler. During his administration one Governor of Madras, Mr. Hollond, and his brother, a Member of Council and Acting Governor, were suspended from office on charges of corruption of the blackest character, and sent to England, the latter in custody.*

But it was precisely in consequence of the successful reforms and more regular organisation introduced by Lord Cornwallis, that the Honourable Company was at last cured of its reluctance to dispense with the existing Native departments, and commenced to introduce, wherever British authority extended, direct management by British officers. Territorial possession was now preferred to the receipt of subsidies. Moreover, with increased power, and closer insight into the condition of the people, a sense of responsibility for the manifold evils under which they laboured, forced itself upon the most able and honest men in the Company's service.

Nowhere were these evils more conspicuous than in the Carnatic. The country was said, and with truth, to be so oppressively and wastefully administered by the Nawab's officers, that the security of the payments due to the Honourable Company was seriously endangered. And thus it had become the leading object with the British Government for several years before the Nawab Wallajah's death, —but more especially since Lord Cornwallis had broken the power of Tippoo in the campaign of 1792,—to obtain the entire civil and military administration of the Carnatic, and to reduce the Sovereign, endowed with a large share of the revenue as his Civil List, to that passive position which was at last produced under the Treaty of 1801. This position was rejected with equal decision by the Nawabs Wallajah and his son Omdut-ool-Oomra, to the great dissatisfaction of the Company, who attributed their obstinate objections to the "perverse counsels" of "interested intriguers." The payment of the subsidy was punctual, affording no pretext for any summary interference.

* *Cornwallis Correspondence*, vol. ii, pp. 64, 81, 112, 327, 482. "10th February, 1791. Letters from Madras mention that Mr. Edward Holland, formerly of Council there, and a few days Acting Governor, was apprehended, in consequence of an order from Government, by an Officer and party of Sepoys, and sent on board the *Rodney* Indiaman, to be conveyed as a prisoner to England." *Selections from the Calcutta Gazettes*, by W. S. Seton-Karr, Esq., (Longman and Co.) vol. ii, p. 285.

On the death of Mahomed Ali Wallajah in 1795, Lord Hobart,* then Governor of Madras, finding the new Nawab Omdut-ool-Oomra quite inaccessible to persuasion on this point, proposed to take the administration of his dominions out of his hands by force. Neither the Governor-General Lord Cornwallis, nor the Court of Directors would agree to so strong a measure; and the difference of opinion on this point led to Lord Hobart's recall.

In 1797 Lord Mornington, afterwards the Marquis Wellesley, was appointed Governor-General, and at the period of his departure the Court of Directors sent a despatch to the Madras Government, from which the following extract is taken:—

"Lord Mornington will render a most essential service to the Company, should he be able to accomplish that object, or an arrangement similar thereto; but feeling, as we do, the necessity of maintaining our credit with the Country Powers by an exact observance of Treaties,—a principle so honourably established under Lord Cornwallis's administration,—we cannot authorise his Lordship to exert other powers than those of persuasion, to induce the Nabob to form a new arrangement."†

In April 1798, Lord Mornington, having arrived at Madras from England, and halting with that express purpose on his way to Calcutta, opened a negotiation with the Nawab with a view to a new Treaty, but "found His Highness," in the words of his despatch to the Court of Directors, "completely indisposed to that arrangement." In April 1799, the Governor-General addressed from Calcutta a long argumentative letter of sixty-two paragraphs to Omdut-ool-Oomra on the same subject; but the Nawab opposed a determined resolution to the modification of the Treaty of 1792.‡

So completely puzzled were all Indian politicians to devise any plan by which the administration could be taken out of the Nawab's hands without an open rupture and a manifest violation of the Treaty, that in 1800 we find even

---

* Afterwards Earl of Buckinghamshire.
† *Carnatic Papers*, 1861, p. 78.
‡ *Ibid.*, pp. 79 to 87; *Wellesley's Despatches*, vol. i, p. 541, and vol. ii, p. 1.

Lord Cornwallis, then Lord-Lieutenant of Ireland, who was consulted on the subject, writing as follows :—

"Mr. Dundas sent me Lord Wellesley's letter, and his answer, and the papers respecting the Nawab of Arcot. I told him that I wished the latter to be so managed as either to frighten him so much as to induce him to give up the management of the country, or to furnish a pretext for taking it from him."*

When a statesman of high honour like Lord Cornwallis, scrupulous even to punctiliousness as to the faith of Treaties, was driven to write in this remarkable style, we may be sure that the condition of Carnatic affairs was becoming very critical. We may assume, also, that not every Anglo-Indian politician was likely to be either as scrupulous or as patient as Lord Cornwallis had been.

The distinguishing peculiarity, augmented at last into an unendurable embarrassment, in our relations with the Nawabs of the Carnatic, arose out of their correspondence with the Royal Family of Great Britain,—an expedient adopted in the times of our earliest and most urgent need, but which by degrees became quite incongruous to the situation, quite inappropriate to the position of the Nawab with reference to the Governor of Madras and the Governor-General.

Until the respective provinces of the Company and the Crown in the Government of India had been clearly defined by the several regulating Acts, and in particular by the Act of 1784, constituting the Board of Control, the strangest confusion and complication of authority frequently occurred. Appeals against the requisitions of the local Government were made by the Nawab to the King, and Ambassadors were sent by his Majesty to his Highness, without the knowledge and in direct defiance of the Honourable Company and its officers in India. Imperial legislation destroyed the legal pretext for this scandalous conflict being openly carried on, but private correspondence not being prohibited it still raged behind the scenes. The exaggerated pretensions were unabated; the antagonism still continued in full force. The following extract from a letter dated the 26th of February, 1796, written by the

* *Cornwallis Correspondence*, vol. iii, p. 289.

Nawab Omdut-ool-Oomra, a few months after his accession, to Lord Cornwallis in England, will show to what a height this antagonism had risen :—

"The uneasiness, vexation, and troubles which I have suffered from the unprovoked and unjust enmity of Lord Hobart, have been such that nothing less than the Divine favour could have supported me under them.

"In the payment of the *kists*" (instalments of the subsidy), "and in all other matters, I have made your Lordship's Treaty my guide, and shall continue to do so, but the disinclination of Lord Hobart towards me is to the present moment unabated. I trust, however, in your Lordship's kindness for my security against every evil, and for the daily increase of my happiness and prosperity. The present situation of affairs gives me much reason for uneasiness and alarm; but, by the blessing of God, I trust in the constant protection of the King of Great Britain, in the generous and humane disposition of the Prince of Wales, and in your Lordship's friendship, for my security and safety. I therefore beg leave to request your Lordship's intercession with His most gracious Majesty and with his Ministers, Mr. Pitt and Mr. Dundas, that orders may be issued that the Company's representatives shall not on any account whatever interfere in my hereditary Government and dominions."*

Besides the complimentary and congratulatory letters on certain established occasions which passed between the Nawab and our Royal Family, we obtain here and there stray hints of other less regular communications, sometimes accompanied by presents. In 1793 we hear of the Nawab sending "two Arabian horses and a young elephant for the King," "eight bales and two horses" for the Prince of Wales.†

Three years later, in 1796, the impropriety and inconvenience of permitting these propitiatory offerings seems to have struck the Ministry, when the practice was extended to themselves, for we find Mr. Dundas addressing Lord Cornwallis on the subject in the following terms:—

"As to the Nabob's horses, I am really as much embarrassed as your Lordship, what it is right to do. The sending the presents is perfectly absurd, and none of us can wish to receive them; but the delicacy I feel about it is how far we can decline them,

---

* *Cornwallis Correspondence*, vol. ii, pp. 322, 323.
† *Ibid.*, vol. ii, p. 553.

without indirectly throwing a blame in a quarter where, as you suppose, I think it is likely they may be accepted."

A note to this page of the *Cornwallis Correspondence* explains that the "quarter" alluded to was the Prince of Wales.

During Lord Wellesley's abortive negotiation three years after the date of the letter last quoted, he found the same obstacles thrown in his way, and was compelled to remonstrate in plain terms against the influence of the British heir apparent:—

"In all his conversations and correspondence he studiously distinguished His Majesty's Government from that of the Court of Directors, uniformly treating the latter with disrespect, and even with ridicule and contempt. In my last conversation with his Highness, he plainly declared to me that he considered His Majesty to be his father, friend, ally, and protector, but that the Court of Directors desired 'to obtain his country anyhow.' The principles of this distinction are encouraged in his Highness's mind by the letters and embassies which have occasionally reached him from His Majesty through channels not only unconnected but avowedly at variance with the British Government in India. All such letters and embassies have the most pernicious tendency to withdraw the confidence and respect of the Natives from the Governments in India, and to fix their attention on His Majesty's naval or military officers, or such person (of whatever character) as may accidentally be the bearers of his letters. The frequent letters which his Highness the Nabob receives from his Royal Highness the Prince of Wales greatly aggravate the same evil; and it is with the utmost concern that I feel myself bound by my public duty to request that you will take an opportunity of representing to his Royal Highness that his correspondence with the Nabob of the Carnatic has produced an effect contrary to his Royal Highness's wishes, and has been highly injurious to the public service in India."†

When matters had arrived at such a pass as this, Lord Wellesley was not the man to allow himself to be baffled, even after two failures. Yet the problem was not easy of solution. The Nawab fulfilled precisely all the conditions of the Treaty. So long as no encroachment was made on his dignity and dominion, he complied with every demand. Even when sulky he was submissive. If for a season he

---

* *Cornwallis Correspondence*, vol. ii, p. 308
† *Wellesley's Despatches*, vol. ii, p. 241.

was on bad terms with a Governor, as in Lord Hobart's time, he was on the best terms, and in close communication, with our Royal Family. There could not be a more difficult personage to deal with.

But while Lord Wellesley was waiting anxiously for the death of the Nawab, Omdut-ool-Oomra, whose health was very precarious, and was maturing a very Oriental scheme for getting up a disputed succession, by originating a doubt, which none of the Wallajah family entertained, as to the legitimacy of the next heir,* a discovery was made, which was at once and with undisguised eagerness seized upon as affording the very pretext wanted for imperiously demanding that the proposals of the British Government should, without reply or discussion, be accepted.

"When the Governor-General, and all his superiors, and all his subordinates, in the Government of India, were languishing and panting for the possession of the Carnatic, but afraid, without some more plausible reason than they yet possessed, to commence the seizure, here it was provided for them in extraordinary perfection. But the very circumstance which recommended it to the eager affections of the East India functionaries, will recommend it to the rigid scrutiny of those whose minds are more happily situated for appreciating the facts."†

And what was this wonderful discovery, brought about, as Lord Wellesley said, by "a combination of fortunate circumstances"?‡ Sir James Fergusson, giving a loose version of the contemporary invective, says, "it was proved that the Nawab of the Carnatic had been in constant communication with Tippoo Sultan, giving him secret information." Mr. Lowe, in the same style, says that "a correspondence of a highly treasonable nature had been carried on in cypher, which proved that the Nawab was one of the allies of Tippoo Sultan."§ The truth is that no correspondence or communication between the Nawabs of the Carnatic and Tippoo Sultan, except the ordinary complimentary letters known to our Government, was ever discovered.

* *Wellesley's Despatches.* vol. ii, p. 249 ; *Carnatic Papers*, 1861, p. 88.
† Mill's *History of India*, 1848, vol. vi, p. 311
‡ *Wellesley's Despatches*, vol. ii, p. 257.   § *Ante*, p. 37.

With the exception of three very harmless and insignificant notes, devoid of anything that could be twisted into a treasonable meaning, one (No. XXI in the Collection*) from a person in the Nawab's household to one of the Mysore officials, and two (No. XVII and No. XX) directed to one of Tippoo's courtiers, signed "Gholam Hoossain," but imputed to the Nawab Omdut-ool-Omra,—all the letters from the Seringapatam archives used as evidence against the Nawabs, were addressed to Tippoo Sultan *by his own servants* employed as Wakeels (Envoys or agents,) at Madras, and describing their interviews with the Nawabs and with certain English officers.

These letters from the Wakeels to their master were treated as if they were exactly equivalent to letters written by the Nawab Wallajah and his son Omdut-ool-Oomra, or their Ministers, to Tippoo Sultan, in defiance of treaty obligations, proving the insincerity of the two Nawabs' attachment to the Company, and constituting them "public enemies."

Every word reported by the Wakeels to Tippoo Sultan is set down by Lord Wellesley as authentic, and as available testimony against the Nawabs; although the Wakeels themselves, in their examination before the Commissioners, admit that in order to gratify their master, the Sultan, they "heightened the expressions" of regard for him that fell from the Nawab Wallajah, as well as those that were uttered by Lord Cornwallis.† And yet if every statement made by Gholam Ali and Ali Reza, Tippoo Sultan's Wakeels, both in their written reports from Madras found among the records at Seringapatam, and in their depositions before the Commission of Inquiry, were to be accepted as truth, it would amount to *nothing*. The proofs of dark designs on the part of the Nawabs are really so frivolous, even if considered as true, that but for Lord Wellesley's strong bias towards any pretext for assuming the administration of the Carnatic, we should be surprised at his not having thrown the whole mass aside, in despair of making a case out of it.

* This collection of documents will be found in the *Carnatic Papers* of 1803, and also in the *Asiatic Annual Register*, 1802, pp. 133 to 146.
† *Asiatic Annual Register*, 1802, p. 180.

It just amounts to this, and to no more, that Tippoo's Wakeels in their written reports to their own master, represent the Nawab Wallajah as dissatisfied with his subordination to the Company, and declare that he constantly complimented Tippoo as a pillar of the Mussulman faith, that he frequently said that all Mahomedans should be united, and that he assured them of his having been personally opposed to the war with Tippoo, which Lord Cornwallis had just brought to a victorious conclusion. Any "treasonable" or hostile character that might attach to these expressions of opinion, if we consider them to be correctly reported, is removed by the fact that the Wakeels represent these identical complaints as having been uttered by the Nawab on more than one occasion in the presence of Lord Cornwallis, General Meadows, and other British officers, one of whom, Major Doveton, is made to corroborate the Nawab's statement without a single word or hint of disapproval. Here is an extract from one of the Wakeels' reports. The Princes therein mentioned are the two sons of Tippoo, who were then residing as hostages at Madras.

"On the 13th of June, 1792, Wallajah, Omdut-ool-Oomra, and Hoossain Nawaz Khan, younger son of Wallajah, Lord Cornwallis and General Meadows, came to visit the Princes. They sat two hours' (about three quarters of an hour English,) 'and talked a great deal with them. His Highness took occasion to observe that we considered him to have been an enemy, whereas he declared in the presence of God, that he was not and is not; that, on the contrary, he was a friend and well-wisher; and that he had opposed the breach between your Majesty and the three allied States to such a degree that every one decided in his own mind that inwardly your Majesty and his Highness were one ; *and he desired us to ask Lord Cornwallis and General Meadows, who were present, whether he said true or not.*"*

In another letter they describe a visit paid by the Princes to the Nawab Wallajah on the 29th of July, 1792, on which occasion the Nawab is said to have reiterated his assurances of admiration and friendship for Tippoo Sultan, and of the opposition he had given to the recent war ; declaring that he had both spoken and written to

* *Asiatic Annual Register* for 1802, p. 134.

Lord Cornwallis "on the subject of making peace," complaining that "his Lordship had uncontrolled authority, and listened to the advice of others," and adding the pious adjuration, " God preserve you and me from the wicked designs of others." This speech, according to the Wakeels, was made in the presence of two British officers, apparently with their concurrence and approval.

"Major Doveton and another officer, being of the party, his Highness appealed to them, observing that they had been present at the time, and could speak to the truth or falsity of what he said. Major Doveton replied that it was very true, and that several English gentlemen were consequently much displeased with his Highness; that one day when his Highness had assembled all the gentlemen, under pretence of giving them an entertainment, but really for the above purpose, and had accordingly suggested pacific measures, the expediency of which he urged in a thousand ways, they were so displeased that they went away without partaking of the entertainment,—nay, that to their animosity might be attributed the assumption of his Highness's country; that when the orders were received from the King of England to restore the country, they framed the pretence among themselves that his Highness was too much attached to Tippoo Sultan."*

Even in the prejudiced description of these documents by the Persian translator to Government, the following remarks are made on this particular despatch :—" In one of the reports of the Wakeels, which contains the substance of a conference between themselves, the Princes and the Nawab, at which Colonel Doveton was present, a speech is ascribed to that gentlemen which is evidently fabricated, a circumstance which tends to weaken the validity of all their reports."† Clearly, if the Wakeels could fabricate a speech for Colonel Doveton, they could fabricate one for the Nawab Wallajah. But the most singular proof of the irresistible bias under which Lord Wellesley and his subordinates were acting, is that if every speech attributed by Tippoo's officers to the Nawabs be taken as a verbatim report, there is nothing disloyal or hostile to the British Government to be found in them. It is only by wresting every high-flown compliment to Tippoo Sultan, and every

---

* *Asiatic Annual Register*, 1802, pp. 135, 136.
† *Wellesley's Despatches*, vol. ii, p. 749.

expression of attachment to the Mussulman faith, into a proposal for alliance in a holy war against all Christians, that the Persian interpreter is enabled to make anything of them at all.

There only remain to be noticed the three notes which are not from the two Wakeels, and the so-called "cypher," to which Mr. Lowe alluded in his speech. One of these notes (No. XXI) is from Khader Nawaz Khan, a confidential servant of high rank in the household of the Nawab Omdut-ool-Oomra, to Gholam Ali Khan, who had been one of Tippoo's Wakeels at Madras. It is endorsed as received at Seringapatam on the 8th of January, 1797. After the usual exordium of compliments and inquiries after health, the only noticeable passage in this letter runs as follows :—

"What you write of the satisfaction of the Nawab Tippoo Sultan Bahadoor, (may his shadow be extended!) upon the intimation of my attachment, has called forth my highest thanks and endless praises; and I beg you will represent my respectful acknowledgments for his kindness and favours towards me. I have been from first to last endeavouring that, through the favour of God, the degree of union between those two chosen of the Lord" (meaning the Nawab Omdut-ool-Oomra and Tippoo Sultan," which is calculated to promote the happiness of God's people, may daily be strengthened and cemented, and mutual friendship and attachment be confirmed and established; and thanks be to the Almighty that the system of harmony and union has acquired the requisite degree of stability and firmness."*

It is to be observed that there is nothing whatever in this very unobjectionable note, despatched when we had been at peace with Tippoo for five years, to show that it bore what we should call an official character, or was written by the Nawab's order. It is evidently a private letter; and Gholam Ali Khan, to whom it was addressed, in his examination before the Commissioners, said that he believed Khader Nawaz Khan, "being a man not very opulent," had sent it in the hope of "obtaining a present from Tippoo Sultan."†

The first of the two letters imputed to the Nawab Omdut-ool-Oomra himself (No. XVII), is described as

* *Asiatic Annual Register*, 1802, p. 146.   † *Ibid.*, p. 187.

written with a pencil on half a sheet of English paper, signed, "Gholam Hoossain," and addressed to Gholam Ali Khan. The most convincing mode of displaying its innocent character is to transcribe the whole of it. It is dated the 12th of August, 1794, when we were at peace with Tippoo, and shortly after the hostage Princes had returned from Madras to Mysore.

"Good faith is the practice of Syuds.* I complain of frequent neglects. Let me be sometimes called to remembrance; at all events the intelligence of the marriage of the Princes has rejoiced me. The presents usual on such occasions from my father will be sent. Repeat the following couplet on my part to the Nawab Tippoo Sultan.

"In the preservation of thy person is the perpetual permanence of the faith.

"Let him not remain who wisheth not thy preservation."
"Make my complaints to his Highness of his not writing to me; if permission be required you will obtain it. To the Princes, respect; to Reza Ali Khan, compliment. Gholam Hoossain."†

The second is said to be "written in the same hand as the Nawab's letters invariably are," signed "Gholam Hoossain," and addressed to Gholam Ali. The date of its receipt at Seringapatam is the 8th of January, 1797, when we were at peace with Tippoo. It runs as follows:—

"After a lapse of time, and the moment my heart was desirous of learning accounts of your health, I had the pleasure to receive your friendly letter; and I was gratified by the news of your welfare. I have fully comprehended the several points contained in that letter. You will become acquainted with the circumstances alluded to from the communications of Mahommed Ghyauss and Mahommed Ghose Khan. Deeming me desirous of receiving the pleasing accounts of your health, you will gratify me by communicating them."‡

The two persons mentioned in this note were Envoys from Tippoo Sultan who had lately left Madras, whither they had been deputed, with the knowledge of our Government, on a special embassy of condolence to the Nawab Omdut-ool-Oomra after his father's death, and of congratulation on his accession to the throne.

* Gholam Ali Khan, whom he was addressing, was a Syud or descendant of the Prophet.
† *Asiatic Annual Register*, 1802, p. 143.   ‡ *Ibid.*, p. 145.

These two notes contain nothing whatever that can render their authorship a matter of the slightest consequence. No provision in the Treaty forbade the Nawab —if these notes were indeed from his hand,—to keep up a private correspondence with any one at Seringapatam, or even with Tippoo Sultan himself. The 10th Article of the Treaty of 1792, which the Nawabs are accused of having violated, contains this provision :—

"The Nawab agrees that he will not enter into any negotiations or political correspondence with any European or Native Power, without the consent of the said Company."*

No effort of ingenuity, or even of imagination, can detect any "negotiations" or "political correspondence," in these two notes.

There now only remains to be considered what is called "*the cypher.*" Mr. Lowe, in his speech of the 13th of June, 1864, said that "a correspondence of a highly treasonable nature had been carried on in cypher."† Any one who will take the trouble to refer to the collection of papers used as evidence against the Nawabs,—in which I have shown that there is nothing "treasonable,"—will find that there is no correspondence at all in cypher among them.‡ There is, however, a paper (No. VI) called "Key to a cypher," said to have been "found among the records at Seringapatam." Trusting to the exaggerated contemporary statements regarding this paper,—the whole affair, we may suppose, not seeming sufficiently important or interesting to repay the trouble of verification,—Mr. Lowe continues :—"Unfortunately for the Nawab the key to the cypher was also found, so that the meaning of the correspondence became known."§ As no part of the correspondence between Tippoo and his Envoys, from which the Nawabs' guilt is assumed, was in cypher, no key was required to make its meaning known. The so-called "Key to a cypher" is merely a list of eighteen proper

* *Collection of Treaties*, Calcutta, 1864, vol. v, p. 243.
† *Ante*, p. 37.
‡ The Wakeels themselves corresponded in cypher once or twice with Tippoo,—in a real cypher composed of numbers,—but no such letter is in the collection; see *Asiatic Annual Register* for 1802, p. 186.
§ *Ante*, p. 37.

names and words, for which certain symbolical terms are to be used in correspondence. Only four of these terms are actually used in the Envoys' letters, and their meaning is rendered so obvious by the context that no key was required to explain them. The Nawab Wallajah in several passages of the Envoys' reports is designated, in accordance with the directions of the Key, "*the well-wisher of mankind.*" Tippoo is called by them, "*the Defender of the Faith.*" Ali Reza, one of the Envoys, is similarly entitled "*the distinguished in friendship.*" The hostage Princes are once spoken of by the term laid down in the Key,—"*hearts.*" Not one of the other symbolical terms is employed in any part of the Envoys' correspondence.

Let me now exhibit the whole of this portentous and "highly treasonable" document.

"Oh God, glorious and exalted! Oh Prophet of God! May the blessing of the Lord be upon him! Religion.

The Nawab Wallajah,	The Nawab Tippoo	Benevolent,
The Friend of Mankind.	Sultan,	*The Hand.*
Ali Reza,	*The Defender of the*	The Heart,
The Distinguished in	*Faith.*	*A Seal.*
friendship.	Nizam-ood-Dowla,	The English.
The Power of God,	*Nothing.*	*The New-comers.*
A Saddle.	The Victorious,	The Mahrattas,
Sons,	*A Scimitar.*	*The Despicable.*
Hearts.	A State or Dominion,	A Present,
	A Ring.	*A Flower.*
	The Faith,	Omdut-ool-Oomra,
	Religion.	*The Restorer of the*
	Gholam Ali Khan,	*Faith.*"*
	Nawab Sahib.	
	The Spring,	
	A flower-garden.	
	A Letter,	
	An Interview.	

It will be seen at once that three of these words convey a meaning which may be considered hostile to the British Government. The English are called "*the New-comers*;" the Nizam, "*Nothing*;" and the Mahrattas, "*the Despic-*

* *Asiatic Annual Register*, 1802, p. 137. I have endeavoured to arrange the words in a more intelligible manner than I found them, but have altered nothing.

able," —these three confederate Powers having subdued
Tippoo in the campaign of 1792 under Lord Cornwallis,
and deprived him of half his dominions. These terms,
however, make their appearance in no other document in
the collection. Then how are the suspicions arising from
this paper, found in Tippoo's archives, fastened upon the
Nawabs of the Carnatic? Because the paper is said to be
endorsed by one of Tippoo's clerks with the words, " the
writing of Omdut-ool-Oomra." The writing is admitted
not to be that of Omdut-ool-Oomra; but this trifling fact
is not allowed to impede the predetermined result. If it
is not the Nawab's writing, it is declared to be that of
his confidential Secretary. One of Tippoo's Envoys, Ali
Reza, in his examination before the Commissioners, states
that this paper was delivered to his colleague at Madras
by Khader Nawaz Khan,—the person already mentioned
as being "not very opulent" and desirous of a present
from Tippoo Sultan,* and that he said it was to be used
"for communication between Tippoo Sultan and the
Nawabs."† It was never so used, but that was of little
consequence. No further trace was found of this terrible
engine of secret correspondence. No search—no discovery
at least—was made in the records of the Nawab at Madras.
No question was put to Khader Nawaz Khan. No Secretary, clerk, or record-keeper in the Nawab's household
was examined. Too close an inquiry might have dispelled the superficial effect of this absurd scrawl, which
may very well have owed its origin to some petty intrigue
between Khader Nawaz Khan—"not very opulent"—and
Tippoo's Envoy, in which the latter may have been the
dupe. Or the two may have been acting in concert, the
one to strengthen his influence with Tippoo, the other to
obtain that present which, we are told, he desired to
obtain.

Yet, although this paper was susceptible of such easy
explanation, without the Nawabs, to whom it was never
traced, being implicated, it is paraded in the following

* *Ante*, p. 57.
† *Asiatic Annual Register*, 1802, pp. 178 and 179.

fashion in the public Declaration issued by the Government of Madras in 1801:—

"A cypher was composed *and actually introduced into the separate and secret correspondence between the Nawabs Mahomed Ali and Tippoo Sultan;* the original Key of the said cypher, discovered among the records of Seringapatam, is in the handwriting of the confidential Moonshee (or Secretary) of the Nawab Mahomed Ali and of the Nawab Omdut-ool-Oomra; and the said cypher was delivered by a confidential agent of the Nawab Omdut-ool-Oomra to the Ambassador of Tippoo Sultan, for the express purpose of being transmitted to Tippoo Sultan."*

A more flagrant exaggeration, a more gross perversion of the truth, could hardly have been concocted. Indeed, enough has been already said to prove that, without the most audacious exaggeration, nothing could have been made of what was called "the documentary evidence." Lord Wellesley himself was not satisfied with it. In a despatch to Mr. Dundas, dated the 5th of March, 1800, mentioning the recent discovery of papers at Seringapatam, he says of the Nawab Omdut-ool-Oomra,

"The proof arising from written documents of his overt acts of hostility since his accession, is not so full and distinct as that which relates to his former agency. But this defect may be supplied by oral testimony, as all the necessary witnesses are alive and in our hands."†

This defect was, however, not supplied. This letter having been written in March, the Commissioners commenced their sittings, held at Vellore and Seringapatam, in May, 1800. In May, 1801, Lord Wellesley communicates to Lord Clive the opinions he has formed on "the oral examinations taken by the Commissioners." "The tendency of those examinations," he continues, "is of a nature, in some important parts of the evidence, rather to weaken than to confirm the impression made on my mind by the written documents."‡

Although he adds, "In other branches of the evidence the oral testimony has served to illustrate and strengthen the proofs afforded by the correspondence," the preceding

* *Asiatic Annual Register,* 1802, p. 129.
† *Wellesley's Despatches,* vol. ii, pp. 246, 247.
‡ *Ibid.,* vol. ii, p. 516.

acknowledgment on the part of one who, like Lord Wellesley, had so obviously come to a foregone conclusion, is very remarkable. It proves that he had not found the confirmation he expected.

In truth the depositions recorded by the Commissioners in their Report, still more their brief notice of other depositions which they considered it useless to record, and even more, perhaps, the fact of their carefully abstaining from examining several persons who, in Lord Wellesley's words, were "in our hands,"—totally dependent on the bounty of our Government,—denote the utter failure of the entire process. No evidence of any secret correspondence between the Nawabs and Tippoo was to be extracted from any one.

The most important of the depositions recorded at full length by the Commission were those of the two Envoys, Ali Reza and Gholam Ali Khan, who, of course, could best elucidate their own correspondence. But, in the words of the historian Mill, "the evidence of both, taken together, tends not to confirm one single suspicion, if any could have been justly derived from the papers, but to remove them, every one."* For instance, great stress is laid by the Persian Interpreter, in his Report, on "*the mysterious expression* so frequently made use of in the correspondence between the Wakeels and Tippoo Sultan, —'*the affair you know of.*'" This, he says, proves that "the Wakeels were charged with *some concealed commission* at Madras." "But what the nature of it was does not clearly appear."†

This, no doubt, was one of the "defects" which Lord Wellesley hoped might "be supplied by the oral testimony." It *was* supplied; the nature of this mysterious affair appeared at once from the evidence of the two Envoys. The mystery was cleared up in a manner most creditable to the Nawabs, and most destructive to the theory of their friendly feelings towards the Sultan of Mysore. "The affair you know of" referred to the project of a marriage between one of Tippoo's sons and a

* *Mill's History*, vol. vi, p. 322.
† *Wellesley's Despatches*, vol. ii, p. 743,—see also 744 and 750.

young lady of the Wallajah family. The proposal was made in the first instance on the part of the Sultan; it was intended to have been effected with the knowledge of the British Government; but "*the Nawab Wallajah was averse to the connection.*"*

The secrecy observed in conducting these negociations was perfectly natural under the circumstances. Besides the reserve always maintained in the earlier stage of such an affair, there were in this particular instance special reasons for keeping the matter quiet. Hyder Ali, Tippoo's father, was of decidedly plebeian origin. Father and son had failed in contracting matrimonial alliances for themselves or their children with any of the old Mussulman houses of India. The Nawab Wallajah boasted of an honourable pedigree irrespective of his sovereignty. A marriage connection with the Carnatic family would have been promotion for Tippoo Sultan. The open rejection of his offer would have been a stinging mortification, injurious to his political influence as well as to his personal dignity.

If the Nawab Wallajah had really wished to establish friendly relations with the Mysore Sultan, and to keep up a secret intercourse with him,—either from hostility to his British allies, or simply with a view to unforeseen eventualities,—there could have been no more convenient chain of communication established than a marriage between the two families. That the Nawab rejected the opportunity of forming such a chain is very strong proof that he wished for no such secret intercourse.

Where there is nothing on the other side but flimsy suspicions and sophistical inferences, it is a work of supererogation to point out the antecedent improbabilities against any cordiality or community of purpose arising between the Nawab and the Sultan. Those improbabilities are overwhelming.

The great Lord Clive in 1765, eighteen years after the first assistance rendered to us by Mahomed Ali Wallajah in person,† described him as "the best Mussulman I ever

---

* *Asiatic Annual Register,* 1802, p. 175.
† *Ante,* p. 41.

knew."* Twenty-two years later, in 1787, Sir Archibald Campbell, Governor of Madras, said :—

"I have narrowly watched the Nawab's conduct and sentiments since my arrival in this country, and I am ready to declare that I do not think it possible that any Prince or person on earth can be more sincerely attached to the prosperity of the Honourable Company than his Highness."†

Warren Hastings, writing to the Court of Directors on the 28th of November, 1783, called him, "the Nawab Wallajah, your old and faithful friend and ally,—an aged Prince, whose life, to the last dregs of it, has been spent in the mutual intercourse of friendship with the Company and the British nation, and in participation of all the vicissitudes which have attended their fortunes."‡

We are called upon to believe that this Nawab Wallajah, in his old age, after fifty years of faithful alliance and friendship with the English, and thirty years of almost incessant warfare with Hyder Ali and Tippoo Sultan, suddenly took it into his head to conspire against his friends of half a century, and to league with his enemies of thirty years. We are called upon to believe that the time chosen for this sudden change of policy was just when the power of his friends was apparently established without a competitor, and when the power of his old enemy had fallen, beneath all hope of recovery. Wallajah and Omdut-ool-Oomra are accused of having begun their hostile intrigues in 1792, after Lord Cornwallis's campaign, when Tippoo had been compelled to cede half his dominions, to pay three millions and a quarter sterling as a war indemnity, and to submit to the humiliating condition of sending two of his sons as hostages to Madras. And it is with Tippoo's Envoys who were sent to Madras in attendance on these young Princes, that the Nawabs are accused of having concerted and carried on the desperate conspiracy with their discomfited foe against their triumphant friends and allies. In addition to the thirty years of warfare, — "the long established rivalry and

* *Carnatic Papers*, 1861, p. 53.   † *Ibid.*, p. 53.
‡ *Papers, East Indian Affairs*, 1806, p. 4; *Carnatic Papers*, 1861, p. 51.

F

enmity between the two families," which the Commissioners admit in one of their questions,*—it must be taken into consideration that both Hyder Ali and Tippoo, especially the latter, had seized every occasion of injuring the Nawab, and of heaping insults upon him. The subservience of the Nawab Wallajah to the East India Company was the constant theme of Tippoo's contempt and ridicule. When Bangalore, the second city in the Mysore territories, where the Sultan had a Palace and sometimes resided, was taken by Lord Cornwallis; a rude fresco picture of large dimensions was found decorating a wall, in which the Nawab Wallajah was represented with a rope round his waist, prostrating himself before an English officer, seated in a chair, who placed one foot upon his neck.†

But a more serious outrage on the family pride of the Nawab Wallajah, and on the tenderest feelings of his nature, had been perpetrated by Hyder and Tippoo, which can never have been forgotten or forgiven. His younger brother, Abd-ool-Wahab, with his entire household fell into the hands of Hyder Ali at the capitulation of the fort of Chandergherry in January, 1782. The Nawab's brother was kept as a prisoner for upwards of two years. The women were all taken into Hyder's harem. Two granddaughters, of tender years when captured, eventually became Tippoo's concubines.‡

The testimony of the two Envoys given before the Commission of Inquiry, all tends to show that the great attention paid by the Nawab Wallajah to the hostage Princes simply arose from the natural kindness and courtesy of his disposition, and that his protestations of friendship for Tippoo Sultan, encouraged by Lord Cornwallis and Sir Charles Oakley, then Governor of Madras, who desired to promote a good feeling at the Mysore Court, were due solely to combined motives of politeness and policy.

One of the Envoys, Ali Reza, besides explaining that

* *Asiatic Annual Register* for 1802.
† *Historical Sketches of Southern India, by Colonel Mark Wilks*, vol. iii, p. 140. ‡ *Ibid.*, vol. ii, p. 350.

it was customary for them in their reports to "heighten the expressions of regard that fell from the Nawab Wallajah, for the purpose of conciliating the mind of Tippoo Sultan," declares his positive opinion that "*there was no sincerity in the Nawab's expressions of friendship.*" He gives his meaning more fully in the following answer to a question put by the Commissioners:—

"The whole is compliment. How is it possible that the Nawab Wallajah could forget the indignities sustained by his own family at the hands of Tippoo Sultan, when Abdool Wahab (the Nawab's brother) was confined, and his daughter and grand-daughter taken into the Mahal."*

In another reply he says:—"It was the language of the tongue, and not of the heart."†

On the other hand, this same Ali Reza, regarding whom the Commissioners say that he evinced "a ready disposition to give the fullest information," and that they discovered in him "no wilful prevarication, or endeavour to suppress the truth,"‡ described in the strongest and most unequivocal language the efforts made by the Nawab Wallajah to persuade Tippoo to give up all thought of renewing a hopeless contest, to keep faith and remain on amicable terms with the British Government. He says that on one occasion the Nawab, "in the most earnest manner, taking God to witness, sent his entreaty to the Sultan, that he should refrain from breaking with the English, and that he should adhere to the friendship established between them."§ All the good counsel verbally transmitted through the Envoys to Tippoo was, he says, "confirmed by the advice of the Nawab Wallajah, founded on his long experience and age."|| On another occasion "the Nawab Wallajah stated that the Sultan should consider the connexion with the English to be *the proper object of his religious care.*"¶

Ali Reza also declared that the Nawab Omdut-ool-Oomra, at the departure of the Wakeels, "directed them

* *Asiatic Annual Register*, 1802, pp. 179, 180.
† *Ibid.*, 1802, p. 181. ‡ *Ibid.*, p. 182.
§ *Ibid.*, p. 175. || *Ibid.*, p. 177.
¶ *Ibid.*, p. 181.

to assure the Sultan of his regard, and to advise him not to break with the English; that he should not consider this communication to be a deviation from the principles of their religion, but that *the true Islam consisted in preserving unity with the English.*"*

Nor can the apologists for the action of Lord Wellesley's Government strengthen their case by discrediting their own witnesses,—by urging that the former Envoys are not to be trusted, when they depose to the loyalty and good faith of the two Nawabs. This position is closed to my opponents, not so much on the technical ground that these are their *own* witnesses, as from the fact that they are *the only witnesses.* The Commissioners laid hands on these men,—Lord Wellesley remarked that they were "in our hands,"—and with the most ostentatious intimidation, and in a series of egregious leading questions, called on them to curse the two Nawabs; and when the process has failed, and naught but blessings have come forth, it is impossible to discard or cry them down, for there are no others to take their places. The Commissioners say, "We examined Gholam Ali Meer Suddoor, the Dewan Poorniah,† and the Moonshee Habeeb Oollah," —that is to say, Tippoo Sultan's most trusted Ministers, the men above all others acquainted with the secrets of his Government,—" but as their testimony did not establish any fact, we thought it unnecessary to record their evidence."‡ Not a single servant of the Nawabs was examined. The historian Mill very fairly sums up the general effect of the case brought forward against the Nawabs in the following words :—

"Not only does this evidence afford no proof of a criminal correspondence with Tippoo on the part of the Nabob, but the total inability of the English to produce further evidence, with all the records of the Mysore Government in their hands, and all the living agents of it within their absolute power, is a proof of the

---

* *Asiatic Annual Register,* for 1802, p. 173.

† Tippoo's chief officer of finance, afterwards well known as Minister of the Rajah of Mysore.

‡ *Carnatic Papers,* 1803, p. 39; *Mill's History,* (edited by H. H. Wilson, 1848) vol. vi, p. 322.

contrary, since it is not credible that criminal correspondence should have existed and not have left more traces of itself."*

One very conclusive proof that Tippoo's Envoys succeeded in establishing no plan of secret correspondence with the Nawabs, and effected nothing of consequence during their mission, consists in the fact that immediately, or very soon after their return from Madras to Seringapatam with the young Princes, they were disgraced, forbidden to appear at the Sultan's Durbar, and were for some time kept in confinement.† Doubtless their great offence was that of having so completely failed in "the affair you know of," the negociation of a marriage.

On the other hand, the tone and tenor of Lord Wellesley's despatches, both before and after the Treaty of 1801, prove two things,—firstly, that there was a settled purpose of assuming the civil and military administration of the Carnatic (as the Nawab Omdut-ool-Oomra said, the Company "desired to obtain his country anyhow"), long before the fictitious revelations of Tippoo's archives; secondly, that the real danger and difficulty to be overcome by the desired transfer of power, was not what is called in India "political" but administrative.

In the first glow of success Lord Wellesley writes as follows to the Secret Committee in a despatch dated the 21st of October, 1801 :—

"It is a great satisfaction to have ultimately accomplished an object, long and earnestly desired by the Honourable Company, and earnestly recommended by the Court of Directors to my special attention, when I had the honour to receive the charge of this Government. Your Honourable Committee is apprised of the early solicitude which I manifested for the accomplishment of this important measure, upon my first arrival in Madras, in April, 1798, as well of the repeated attempts which I made on various occasions, in the years 1798 and 1799, to effect the same salutary arrangement. The successive failure of these attempts, combined with the reflections arising from the equally unpropitious result of every preceding proposition of a similar nature, have enhanced, in my mind, the pleasure of witnessing the conclusion of the late Treaty."

* *History*, edited by *Wilson*, 1848, vol. vi, p. 322.
† *Asiatic Annual Register* for 1802, pp. 177, 178 and 187.

He does, indeed, mention in this despatch "the treachery and ingratitude of their late Highnesses, the Nawabs Wallajah and Omdut-ool-Oomra," but more as an opportunity gained than as a danger avoided; for he congratulates the Honourable Committee on the fact that "the possession of the records of the House of Hyder Ali," " is the source from which we have derived that information *which has enabled us to complete the settlement of the Carnatic.*" And then observe what are the good results expected from this "salutary arrangement."

"The union of all local authorities, and the extinction of every principle of conflicting power, will preclude the operation of those causes of discord and counteraction which must ever have impeded the progress of good government in the Carnatic, while the administration of affairs continued in the hands of the Nawab."*

Making the most liberal and charitable allowances for self-deception on the part of all those engaged, it is transparently obvious that the retrospective charge of treason was a mere piece of machinery, employed to effect a predetermined removal with the least possible amount of noise and friction.

The British authorities in 1801 knew very well,—as my quotations will have made manifest,—that in their control of the Nawab they had been thwarted and embarrassed, not by any secret intercourse with the Sultan of Mysore, but by constant private correspondence with the Prince of Wales. The Nawab's intrigues had been carried on by Englishmen in London, not by Mahomedan emissaries in India. It was against this substantial grievance they wished to guard, not against imaginary plots with Native Princes.

A very fair description of the overpowering motives, and the feeling of irresponsible isolation, under which Lord Wellesley and his subordinates acted, is given in two passages of his great work, by the philosophical historian, James Mill.

In the one passage, while giving Lord Wellesley credit for "conspicuous virtues," he speaks of "the violence with

* *Wellesley's Despatches*, vol. ii, pp. 590, 591.

which he was apt to desire, and the faculty which he possessed of persuading himself, that everything was righteous by which his desires were going to be fulfilled."*

In the other he observes :—

"Not only are the English rulers in India deprived of the salutary dread of the scrutinising minds and free pens of an enlightened public, in the regions in which they act ; they well know that distance and other circumstances so completely veil the truth from English eyes, that if the case will but bear a varnish, and if they take care to stand well with the Minister, they have in England everything to hope, and seldom anything to dread, from the successful gratification of the passion of acquiring."†

The best explanation and palliation of the very questionable extremities to which the authorities in India were driven, is that they were so completely bewildered by the difficulties of dealing with the Nawab, as to be irresistibly predisposed to fly to any belief and any line of conduct that promised them immediate relief. The actual situation was intolerable.

Never was there such a provoking array of anomalies. To no Prince had such deference been paid; no Prince was kept under such strict surveillance. He resided in Madras, beyond the limits of his own Government, within British jurisdiction though exempt from it, surrounded by British troops, unable to stir hand or foot without permission, and yet exercising despotic power over millions of subjects who had learned to look to the British Government for protection. We were dependent on the revenue of the Carnatic for the support of all our establishments in the South of India ; yet we were compelled to see the Nawab destroying the resources of the country before our face, for the benefit of the birds of prey of all nations, who flattered and fleeced him.‡ Advice

---

* *History*, vol. vi (1848), p. 312. † *Ibid.*, vol. vi, 1848, p. 323.

‡ Such was the official account, and doubtless there was a great deal of truth in it; and for our purpose it is even more to the point that such was the strong and sincere official belief. Still, when we did take possession, we found, as we did in Oude, that the country was not in the ruined condition we had imagined, and that the British Collectors were not eagerly hailed by the population as their deliverers from oppression.

and remonstrance were obstinately rejected; and when pressed very closely by the Governor of Madras or the Governor-General, he reviled the Honourable Company, and invoked their master, his friend and constant protector, the King of Great Britain.*

He could not be treated like the Nawab-Nazim of Bengal, who had been finally put on the shelf ever since 1772. The Nawab-Nazim was really a creature of our own. We had set up and pulled down, and restored several of them. Not only had the Bengal Nawab never been recognised as a Sovereign by any one, and never pretended to be an independent Ruler, but from the year 1765 he had lost even his nominal share in the duty of public administration. The Company having been confirmed by the Emperor's grant in the Dewannee of Bengal, including the right of assessing and expending the revenue, the Nawab's titular rank was merely that of Nazim or military Governor, a designation simply ridiculous when every post of importance was occupied by the Company's troops, and the Nawab's army consisted of a mob of tawdry ragamuffins.

On the other hand, the Nawab of the Carnatic was no creature of ours; and, as we have seen already, we owed much more to him than he owed to us. The first of the family had not to thank us for his elevation, though he fell in battle fighting against the French in our quarrel. As the consequence of our complete success, partly due to his aid and influence, his son had, indeed, sunk to a secondary position in power compared to ourselves. But the recognition of his Sovereignty was complete. His alliance had been eagerly sought by France. Louis XV had sent him the portraits of himself and his Queen. He had adhered steadily to our side. We had negotiated his independence both of the Nizam and the Emperor; and his Sovereignty in the Carnatic was acknowledged by a European Treaty.

No Prince of India but the Nawab of the Carnatic, was ever admitted to the honour of direct correspondence with the King of Great Britain. While most other Na-

* *Ante*, p. 52.

tive Princes were saluted with the number of guns allowed to Governors or Generals, he was received everywhere with a royal salute. All the honours and prerogatives of royalty were achieved by him, or thrust upon him by the British Government. The problem of his peaceful deposition was absolutely insoluble. He could be neither persuaded nor coerced by any regular process. It was a complete dead-lock, and there was no hope of escaping from it by fair means.

Really, if we had not been so hampered by the external jealousies and internal disturbances already mentioned,* it might have been seriously debated whether it would not be the shortest, simplest, and most humane plan, *to declare war*,—to march two Battalions into the grounds of Chepauk Palace, and compel the Nawab Omdut-ool-Oomra to submit to something like the terms that were ultimately imposed on his nephew by the Treaty of 1801. Such a proceeding would have been more in accordance with the forms of International Law, more straightforward and more dignified, than that which was actually adopted.

Still, after the lapse of half a century, no one would have quarrelled with the expedient, if the result, in which every one acquiesced, had not been rudely disturbed. The discreditable details, on which we have been forced to dwell, were not raked up by me, but by those who carried out, and those who defend, the disinheritance, pillage and defamation of his Highness Prince Azeem Jah.

It is easy to understand why the Indian authorities of 1856, and their Parliamentary apologists down to 1865, revive these frivolous charges against the Wallajah family. Their instinct is the same as that which impelled the original performers of 1801. They wish to disguise political ingratitude and cruelty by blackening the unfortunate victim.

He may well be called unfortunate, for the disinheritance of Prince Azeem Jah was really a piece of bad luck. He would most assuredly have succeeded to the musnud of the Carnatic if his nephew had lived two or three years longer. No dethronement would have been proposed

* *Ante*, p. 17.

during the convulsions of 1857. Any handle for a "lapse" would have been seized in 1855 or 1856.

For example,—no one can doubt that if the Nawab-Nazim of Bengal had happened to die within the last two or three years of Lord Dalhousie's administration, that dignity would have been brought to an end,—the family of Moorshedabad would have been handed down the first great step towards that dead level, where, in the accepted formula of the schools, they might "learn to mingle with the people." No one can doubt that in some snug pigeon-hole of the Calcutta Foreign Office, or in some locked portfolio of the Viceroy's cabinet, there lies a " very full, exhaustive and elaborate Minute," marking down the Nizamut of Bengal as a nuisance to be abated on the first vacancy. If there could be any doubt on the subject, we may point to the fact that Lord Dalhousie left on record his proposals for the annexation of Mysore at the death of the reigning Rajah,* and for abolishing the throne of Delhi on the first demise of the Crown.† The Nawab of Bengal was a dignitary of much smaller consequence and much larger income than either of these; he was more closely in contact with the Governor-General, and had been brought under his unfavourable notice by a scandalous affair to which we shall have occasion shortly to refer. The last two Treaties with the Nawabs of Bengal, those of 1766 and 1770, are distinctly "personal" Treaties, containing no mention of "heirs and successors."‡

The *Friend of India*, "Lord Dalhousie's organ,"§ has

---

* *The Mysore Reversion*, (2nd Edition) p. 41.

† *Minute by the Marquis of Dalhousie*, (*Parliamentary Papers*) 1856, para. 41, p. 11; *Retrospects and Prospects of Indian Policy*, p. 251.

‡ *Collection of Treaties*, (Calcutta) vol. i, pp. 66, 69. As personal Treaties they were, according to what I believe to be the only sound and just doctrine, intended to secure all their benefits to the *family* of the weaker contracting party, (see *ante*, pp. 8, 9) but this view was not accepted at Calcutta in 1856, nor has it, I fear, been as yet authoritatively laid down for the guidance of the Indian Foreign Office.

§ " The Serampore weekly paper, the *Friend of India, which was Lord Dalhousie's organ*, and is conducted with great ability, is a perfect Filibuster. Almost every number contains a clever article on the duty of absorbing Native States, resuming jaghires, etc." (Sir Henry Lawrence in 1856.)—*Kaye's Lives of Indian Officers*, vol. ii, p. 314.

repeatedly given forth its penny-trumpet sound in favour of extinguishing "the mock-royalty" of Moorshedabad; and for some years the menaces of this journal—still existing on the strength of its official connections,—were regarded, with good cause, as infallibly portentous.

If the Bengal Nawabship, with its annual revenue of £160,000, never became the predetermined object of retrenchment in the eyes of Lord Dalhousie's Government, the oversight was miraculous.

The good fortune of the Nawab-Nazim of Moorshedabad was not confined to his merely *living* through the Reign of Terror for Native Princes, between 1848 and 1856: the Rebellion of 1857, which delayed Prince Azeem Jah's appeal, and diverted attention from it, afforded the Bengal Nawab an occasion for regaining credit and favour with the Government of India. In 1853 a cruel beating had been inflicted on a man, from the effects of which he died, within the camp of the Nawab of Bengal, though not by his order. His Highness had jurisdiction in those precincts, was responsible for the acts of his retainers, and had not, in the opinion of the Governor-General, taken proper steps on the crime becoming known to him. For this culpable conduct certain penalties and restrictions were imposed upon the Nawab, and his salute of guns was reduced from nineteen to thirteen. During the crisis of 1857 his Highness rendered valuable assistance to the cause of order, not only by exerting his general influence to quell excitement and maintain allegiance, but by placing a large number of elephants at the disposal of Government, and lending the services of his armed followers and confidential officers, at a time when trustworthy Native agency was urgently required and not easily procured. As a reward for these good offices Lord Canning relieved the Nawab from the penal restrictions of 1853, and his public honours and privileges were restored to the old standard.*

Prince Azeem Jah had no elephants to lend us in 1857, for all the stud and equipages of his nephew, whose heir

* *Papers, Honours, and Rewards to Native Princes*, (No. 77, Lords) 1860, pp. 156, 164.

he was, and to whom he ought to have succeeded, had been sold by auction in the previous year, and the proceeds of the sale appropriated by our Government. But all that was in his power he did. In a despatch dated July 7th, 1858, the Court of Directors mentioned as one reason for increasing the stipend offered to Prince Azeem Jah, "the influence of his name and position over the numerous Mahomedan population of Madras, and the excellent conduct of that population during our recent difficulties."*

Lord Harris, indeed, the Governor of Madras, having advised the Prince's disinheritance, both of the sovereignty and revenue and of the real and personal property belonging to the family, and having failed to induce the Prince to abandon his rights and accept the pension offered him, expressed his opinion in a Minute of September 14th, 1858, that "the conduct of the Prince was subject to reprehension," because "the servants of his establishment were allowed to go about begging, apparently in a state of starvation, and he himself was supposed to be equally ill off."

"The Chepauk Agent called on me to report this, and to state that he was fearful lest considerable excitement, if not worse, should ensue; the Commissioner of Police corroborated his statement, and the Agent was desirous of ascertaining whether he should address Government on the subject.

"I considered this course objectionable, and preferred that he should have a private interview with the Prince, and should call his attention, that seeing what was occurring, his conduct in not drawing his allowance could not be considered friendly.

"The Prince in no way changed his course of action after this communication."†

Lord Harris complains that his Highness "manifested so little courtesy and consideration, at a time when it was manifest that it was of importance to keep down all excitement." His lordship's demands for all that can "be considered friendly," "courteous" and "considerate," appear somewhat one-sided. He seems to expect from this Mussulman Prince much more than Christian forgiveness, goodwill and charity. Not only ought he to submit patiently

* *Carnatic Papers*, 1861, p. 8. † *Ibid.*, p. 10.

to his deposition and spoliation, but he and his followers, "to keep down excitement," ought to have appeared quite jolly under the circumstances. If there were any "starvation," it ought to have been kept out of sight.

Lord Harris argues that if Prince Azeem Jah had consented to draw his allowance, and pay his retainers, such a "course would in no way have compromised the claims he was urging." We shall see, however, that on two subsequent occasions he was officially declared to have compromised his claims, and to have "*accepted his position,*" by the very fact of having *accepted two invitations to public balls* given by the Governor of Madras! He was quite right, therefore, in standing on his own resources as long as he could. He was fairly starved out at last, and commenced to draw his stipend, under protest, in 1863.

One of Lord Harris's colleagues in Council, who had borne no part in preventing Prince Azeem Jah's succession,—Mr. (now Sir) Walter Elliot (K.C.S.I.)—recorded the following views:

"The conduct of the Prince, so far as I am aware, has been simply that of a man suffering under severe disappointment, and striving by legitimate applications in those quarters to which an appeal properly lay, to obtain redress.

"There is no question that the Mahomedan population of Southern India shared largely in the excitement caused by the events of last year: it would have been singular if they had not. Nor would it have been very surprising if many of them had taken an active and a hostile part, had the peace of the country been broken. No doubt the precautionary measures adopted by the Right Honourable the President tended very materially to preserve tranquillity, and to restrain the evil designs of the ill-disposed. But I have no reason to believe that the Prince should be included in this number: on the contrary, all his proceedings have been marked by moderation, and by a retiring, submissive spirit.

"The Court have probably felt that *the quiet demeanour of the Mahomedans was owing to Azeem Jah's personal influence. Doubtless his example has not been without its effect;* but his weight with his fellow-countrymen is not great; and I feel confident that whatever evil counsels were debated in Triplicane," (the Mussulman quarter of Madras,) "originated with persons over whom he had no influence, and with whose proceedings he was little acquainted."*

* *Carnatic Papers*, 1861, p. 7.

Of course the "evil counsels *originated* with persons over whom" the Prince "had no influence," but how was it that those persons found it impossible to extend and combine their conspiracies outside their own circle, and to rally the Mussulman population to their side ? Because they immediately encountered the Prince's influence and example. Sir Walter Elliot admits that " his example. was not without its effect," but thinks " his influence" was " not great." It was sufficient.

There is little difficulty in divining the sentiments of the other Councillor, the late Mr. Morehead, afterwards Governor of Madras, from the following paragraph of his very brief Minute on the same occasion. It is hardly necessary to add that he also had not been a member of the Government when the decree of confiscation went forth.

"I make no comments on the previous acts of Government, but I strongly object to any proceedings being now adopted that may tend to counteract the present desire of the Court to ameliorate, in some degree, the position to which Prince Azeem Jah has been reduced."*

Lord Harris had advised the abolition of the Nawabship of the Carnatic, because, in his opinion, " a Court at the Presidency, though destitute of authority and power, must be inimical, or at all events discontented, and capable of being made a nucleus for intrigue."†

The results, as described by himself and his colleagues in the Government of Madras, can hardly be said to have justified his policy or to have verified his expectations. The " nucleus for intrigue" was not found at the Nawab's Court, but, according to Sir Walter Elliot, among " persons over whom the Prince had no influence, and with whose proceedings he was little acquainted."

What a spectacle of Imperial Government for the edification of India and the world ! Well may Sir George Clerk have said that " it is the inconsistency, caprice and mutability of our opinions regarding all great principles that is the bane of our supremacy in India."‡ What must

---

* *Carnatic Papers*, 1861, p. 8.   † Minute, par. 53; *Ibid.*, p. 13.
‡ *Papers, Chiefship of Bughat*, 1854, p. 8.

be the conclusions of any intelligent Native or inquisitive foreigner, after comparing our treatment of the Carnatic family with that which has fallen to the lot of the Nawabs of Bengal? What must they think of our statesmanship, when great dignities are seen to be pulled down or propped up, great dotations confiscated or continued, according to no principles, legal or moral, but by sheer haphazard? What must they think of our justice and discrimination, when they see the Nawab of Bengal, by the mere accident of living over the last year of one Viceroyalty, carry his family and fortunes into a secure harbour, purge himself of old stains, and pluck renewed honours; while Prince Azeem Jah, free from all stain personally and ancestrally, representing old ties and obligations of glaring notoriety, and rendering similar, if less conspicuous, services in the hour of need as his fortunate compeer of Bengal, reaps nothing but a fresh crop of taunts and calumnies? The fable of the Wolf and the Lamb has been played over and over again in our dealings with the Wallajah family. When Prince Azeem Jah is to be robbed of his patrimony, and when that iniquity is to be defended in the House of Commons, the old charges of treason that were used to extort the Treaty of 1801, and which we have already examined, are reproduced to prejudice his cause; and new imputations of "profligacy" and "want of principle,"—some utterly unfounded, all wholly irrelevant,—are cast upon him and his predecessor, the late Nawab, to destroy public sympathy, and divert attention from the legal and political merits of the case. But perhaps it was the unkindest cut of all when Lord Harris, refusing to give Prince Azeem Jah the credit of those good intentions which his colleagues in Council and the Court of Directors were willing to recognise, declared that he was deserving of "reprehension," and "could not be considered friendly," because his servants looked hungry, and "he himself was supposed to be equally ill off."

Lord Harris carried out the Carnatic confiscation under the dominant influence of Lord Dalhousie, who, on receiving at his residence on the Neilgherry Hills, within the Madras Presidency, the intelligence of the late Nawab's death, at once suggested that there was "no direct heir;" that "the future disposal of the title of Nawab of the Carnatic must be the subject of grave consideration;" and that, therefore, "the Government of Madras should not recognise anyone, or permit anyone to represent himself as successor."* The views and expectations of the Governor General could not well be misunderstood after this. As soon as possible he came down from the Hills, took his seat in person at the head of the Madras Council table, and "conferred with the Government of Fort St. George regarding the measures to be adopted."†

Sir Charles Wood, now Lord Halifax, who we shall find to have indicated very clearly his extreme distaste for this case, was not President of the Board of Control at this time. That office was then filled by Mr. Vernon Smith, now Lord Lyveden, who never seems to have ventured to do more than to register, without remark, all Lord Dalhousie's decrees, one after the other.‡ Sir Charles Wood subsequently had a splendid opportunity of reconsidering the question, as he had also with regard to Mysore; but, after manifest hesitation, he threw them both away. Perhaps he had been too long in power. The habits of office and the amenities of party, may have combined to deter him from breaking the continuity of his own proceedings with those of a predecessor who had been a colleague and was still an auxiliary. He may also have met with resistance from other members of the Government.

Sir Charles Wood was questioned on this subject for the first time on the 25th of July, 1861, shortly after his

---

* *Carnatic Papers*, 1860, p. 17.   † *Ibid.*, pp. 38 and 47.

‡ It is supposed that he was placed there by Lord Palmerston in order that Lord Dalhousie, then in the height of his fame, and who was determined to have his own way, should be secure from all interference, either of the Court of Directors, or of the permanent Secretaries of the Board of Control.

accession to the office of Secretary of State for India, by Mr. Layard, M.P. for Southwark, who applied some very strong terms to the conduct of the East India Company. Sir Charles Wood, in reply, said that "the case of Azeem Jah had been referred to the Government of Madras. He concurred generally with the remarks of the honourable Member, and was quite willing to inquire fully into the merits of the case."*

And it is remarkable that in the despatch of the 8th of April, 1862, in which, to use his own cautious words, he declines "to disturb the decision arrived at six years ago," Sir Charles Wood seems carefully to avoid adopting that decision unreservedly as his own, declaring it to have been equitable or stamping it with his approval. He recapitulates the grounds on which that decision had been based by "the Government of India and the Home Authorities," makes no comment, adds no confirmation of his own, but is of opinion, "after a very full, patient, and searching revision of all the papers of this case, and of the arguments adduced by the Memorialist," that "there are no grounds to justify me in disturbing the decision arrived at six years ago."†

During the discussion in the House of Commons on the 26th of February, 1863, raised by the motion of the Right Honourable H. Baillie, M.P. for Inverness-shire, in favour of Prince Azeem Jah's claims, Sir Charles Wood seized the occasion of observing that "what had been done took place in 1855, long before he acceded to his present office."‡

In the debate of the 13th of June, 1864, on Mr. Smollett's motion for a Select Committee, Sir Charles Wood and all the members of the Government refrained from speaking; and in the discussion which followed on the adroit manœuvre by which a division was hastily and unexpectedly snatched, Sir Charles Wood appears to have rejoiced once more in the opportunity of stating that "all

* *Hansard*, vol. clxiv, p. 1508.
† This despatch has been published, but not in any Parliamentary Return,—see Appendix A.
‡ *Hansard*, vol. clxix, p. 816.

G

the transactions to which reference had been made, took place before he became Secretary of State for India."*

It is worthy also of remark that in all the debates on the Carnatic question, Sir Charles Wood has confined himself pretty closely to treating the extinction of the Nawabship as an accomplished fact and as a matter of policy, declaiming against the disadvantages and anomalies of such an institution, but slurring over and setting aside those sophistical arguments as to the rights derived from the alleged misconduct of Prince Azeem Jah's ancestors, by which Mr. Lowe, Sir James Fergusson, and others, had attempted to make out a justification. In the debate of the 14th of March, 1865, on the motion of Sir Fitzroy Kelly, Sir Charles Wood spoke as follows :—

"The honourable and learned gentleman (Sir Fitzroy Kelly) had stated that the reason why Azeem Jah was deprived in 1855 of the position which his predecessors held, was the imputed treason of Wallajah and Omdut-ool-Oomra at the close of the last century; but it was no such thing. The reason for the course taken in 1855 was not any that had been alleged by the honourable and learned gentleman : it was a reason of policy. The mischief of different kinds that had resulted from the maintenance of these mock royalties was the real and valid objection to them. Lord Harris stated the reason as shortly and as clearly as man could state it."†

In the previous debate of the 26th of February, 1863, he had spoken to much the same effect.

"Lord Harris said he was convinced that a serious moral evil was caused by the continuance of this semblance of the pomp and state of an effete Royalty, which, while it did no good to these persons themselves, was capable of being made the nucleus of intrigue."‡

Some one ought to have reminded Sir Charles Wood of the striking contradiction to all the alarms and prognostications of Lord Harris in 1855, afforded by the facts and events of 1857. There was no "nucleus of intrigue" observed in connection with the family of the Bengal Nawab, nor of another stipendiary Prince, the Rajah of Benares. On the contrary, valuable aid and moral support were

* *Hansard*, vol. clxxv. † *Ibid.*, vol. clxxvii, p. 1709.
‡ *Ibid.*, vol. clxix, p. 815.

given to us by both during the severe trial to which the levelling system advocated by Lord Harris was so speedily subjected. The same must be said of the Bhonsla family of Nagpore during the same great crisis. The same must be said of Prince Azeem Jah and his relatives. During fifty-five years' experience of the Treaty of 1801 no "nucleus of intrigue" had ever been detected or suspected at the Nawab's Court. No "nucleus of intrigue" was found in the remnant and faded semblance of a Court kept up by Prince Azeem Jah.

The only part of the Prince's conduct which Lord Harris insists was open to "reprehension," and "could not be considered friendly," was that he declined to compromise his claims by "drawing his allowance," so that his servants were apparently reduced to "a state of starvation."

On the other hand, Sir Walter Elliot declares the Prince's conduct to have been "simply that of a man suffering under severe disappointment;" pronounces all his proceedings to have been "legitimate," "marked by moderation, and by a retiring, submissive spirit," and believes that "his example has not been without its effect" in keeping the evil-disposed Mahomedans quiet.*

Although Lord Harris declined to acknowledge any obligation to Prince Azeem Jah for his good influences over the Mahomedan population, he at least bears testimony to such influence having been urgently required. In this same Minute he says that "during the existence of the troubles,"

"From all the information I was able to obtain, my opinion is that the Mussulmans of Madras were as hostile to our rule as any others of their creed in India. We had many reasons to believe that they were in constant communication with the ill-disposed at Bangalore, Hyderabad, Kurnool, and Trichinopoly; at one time a considerable number endeavoured to get into the town from the neighbouring districts, fully armed; but on their being almost invariably stopped and disarmed by the Police, they gave up that plan. We knew of prayer-meetings being held at the houses of two or three of their principal men, for the purpose of calling down the wrath of Heaven on the infidels, and success to the

* *Ante*, p. 77.

Mussulman arms. We know that the tone of conversation of all classes of their population was most inimical."*

Lord Harris, not seeing, perhaps, how it tells against himself, betrays, also, the fact that one great cause to which this inimical feeling among the Carnatic Mahomedans was attributed by those best capable of judging, was his own treatment of Prince Azeem Jah. He was informed by the Chepauk Agent and the Commissioner of Police, the men in immediate communication with all the sources of intelligence, that they were "fearful lest considerable excitement, if not worse, should ensue," in consequence of the rumours afloat as to the distress in the Prince's household.†

So unreasonable and malignant was the fanaticism of these Southern Mahomedans, that they harboured disloyal thoughts when their social and spiritual Chief was rejected, degraded, and plundered.

Lord Harris himself was so far anxious on this point that he remonstrated with the Prince, and suggested to him that the visible starvation of his servants "could not be considered as friendly." That was his sole complaint against Prince Azeem Jah.

The useful services rendered to us by the fortunate Nawab of Bengal, and the good conduct and influence of the unfortunate Nawab (*de jure*) of the Carnatic, as described by Lord Harris himself and his colleagues in the Madras Government, contradict his Lordship's unfounded surmise that these princely families must be "inimical." By his own account "the considerable excitement, if not worse" among the Mussulman population, was caused by the persecution, not by the maintenance, of "the Court at the Presidency," which he said was sure to be "a nucleus of intrigue." Everything contradicts the notion that Prince Azeem Jah was "inimical," though Lord Harris and Lord Dalhousie had certainly done their best to make him so. I am afraid it may be assumed that the Prince was guilty of being "discontented," but he did not despair,—he has never despaired,—and therefore the conservative traditions and instincts of his family kept him

* *Carnatic Papers*, 1861, pp. 9, 10. † *Ante*, p. 76.

and his relatives true to the spirit of the long standing alliance, which the stronger party had contemptuously repudiated.

It never seems to have struck Lord Harris that people were more likely to be "inimical and discontented," when badly off and badly treated, than when they were well off and well treated. It never seems to have struck him that the Mahomedans of the Carnatic were not likely to become more loyal and less fanatical, when they saw their hereditary Prince, the lawful Head of their creed and community, disowned and insulted, expelled from his Palace, and stripped of his property, by the Allies who, according to popular belief, and in the words of a Governor of Madras, "owed their existence in the East" to the Nawab's ancestors.*

Lord Harris thinks that in 1857 the "Mussulmans of Madras were as hostile to our rule as any others of their creed in India."† Did he suppose that they had become less hostile, or does any one suppose that they are less hostile now, since the degradation and impoverishment of Prince Azeem Jah?

Are there not some reasons to believe that such a population would be more easily kept in order, guided into useful courses, and trained into a higher civilisation, while their director and leader was contented, prosperous, and harmoniously associated with our Government, than when he is ruined and rejected, filled with the bitter consciousness of ill-usage, and rudely thrown back for counsel and sympathy upon his exasperated relatives and retainers? It is on stuff like this that Mahomedan fanaticism, intrigues, and conspiracies are fed and thrive, and not upon "the pomp and state of Royalty," as Lord Harris imagined.

It is a matter of no small political importance to keep the Mahomedan population of Southern India in good heart, and under effective moral control, convinced of British honour as well as of British power, yielding willing allegiance to the Crown, and intelligent obedience to the laws. Nothing teaches and impresses like example.

* Ante, p. 44. † Ante, p. 83.

Nothing was so calculated to preserve Mussulman allegiance, as the sight and example of their Nawab, honoured and favoured by the Imperial Government. Nothing was so calculated to impress them with respect for laws and contracts, as the example of a powerful Government like ours, evincing a scrupulous respect for treaties and engagements, even with the weakest of its Allies. The statesmanship of 1855 has taught them a very different lesson.

The historical antecedents and social energy of the Mahomedan tribes, entitle them to greater weight and greater consideration among the constituent elements of the Indian population, than might seem warranted by their actual numbers. They congregate in the large towns and cities; and comparatively a small proportion of their creed is to be found among the lowest and most ignorant class of agriculturists and labourers. The point of honour is strong among them. Their faculty of combination and of organisation under a chosen leader, is greater than that of the Hindoos. Their political influence has never died away; and everywhere a certain undefinable deference is still shown by all classes of the community to a Mahomedan of respectable standing.

In Southern India,—the Deccan and the Carnatic,—particular attention is due to the views and sentiments of the Mussulman population, because, in addition to other reasons, they furnish far more than their due share of recruits, and the absolute majority of Native commissioned and non-commissioned officers, to the Madras Army. That Army (and the same may be said of the Hyderabad Contingent) is animated and swayed by Mussulman feelings and traditions.

Just as it has become the fashion, even among those whose duty it is to be well informed on these points, to set down the inhabitants of the Madras Presidency in general as a spiritless and pusillanimous race, so it seems to be taken for granted that the Madras Sepoys, having, with the exception of one Cavalry Regiment, behaved well in 1857, are a quiet, orderly set of fellows, who take no interest in political events, and that since the mutiny of Vellore in 1806, which was brought about by an imprudent provocation, there has been no reason to doubt their loyalty to the Government, and their attachment to their officers. I have endeavoured to shake the delusion as to the fighting capabilities of the South by recalling some almost forgotten incidents of the Polygar war.* I might easily, also, adduce a chain of incidents to show the false estimate that has been formed of the temper and latent motives of the Madras troops, including the detection of a great military conspiracy with marked political aims at Bangalore in 1832, when four of the ringleaders were blown from guns, and two were shot, besides several minor mutinies since that time ostensibly about pay, marches, and other alleged grievances.

It is true that the Madras Army behaved well in 1857: both the men and their officers deserve much more credit and honour than they got, for their excellent state of discipline and their good conduct in the field and in quarters, during the time of trial. But it would be absurd to fall into dreams of fancied security, either about them or the Punjaubees,—commonly called in England the "Sikh" Regiments, and supposed to be recruited from the tribes of that creed, who in fact, though giving a certain character and spirit to the battalions in which they serve, do not contribute more than twenty per cent. to their numerical strength.

"We shall profit, if we are wise, by the counsel which the late Rajah of Puttiala, our faithful ally, and himself a Sikh, addressed to Mr. Raikes:—'Wait, sir, till this excitement of victory, this surfeit of plunder, be over; wait till you mass large bodies of Sikhs in your cantonments; and then remember that I warned you of the danger.'

"Mr. Raikes proceeds:—'This conversation made the greater impression on me, as comprising the views of Brigadier Chamberlain, who a few days before had said to me: 'The Sepoys have waited a hundred years to mutiny; the Sikhs, if subject to like temptations, will not wait ten.' He also had received from the Rajah of Jheend (a Sikh) a similar warning."†

The Punjaub Force is Sikh. The Bengal Army was Brahmin. In the same sense, the Madras Army is Mussulman.

* *Ante*, pp. 18 to 20. † *Edinburgh Review*, October 1866, p. 340.

The Mahomedans take the lead and give the general tone to the Army. One-third of the Madras Infantry, nearly the whole of the Cavalry, and more than half of the Native Officers and Sergeants, are Mahomedan. That peculiar element in the population of India has never been supposed to be less inflammable than the Hindoo element.

It may be mentioned here that Syud Ahmed, the fanatic leader of a religious invasion of the Punjaub, which gave Runjeet Sing much trouble in 1835, and founder of the Wahabee colony in Sitana, which gave us so much trouble in 1858 and 1863,* came from Arcot, the district which furnishes a large proportion of Mussulman recruits for the Madras Army,—a fact worthy of notice, both as indicating the latent capabilities of the population from which that remarkable man sprang, and also as giving a hint of the strange and unaccountable connection and communication between the most distant parts of India, which circumstances every now and then reveal.

Still, any one who pleases may believe, though I cannot, that the Madras Sepoy is made of a different clay from the high-caste Poorbeeas who filled the Bengal Army, that he is a tame creature of domestic habits, and totally devoid of ambition, or that he is deeply convinced of the blessings of British rule, and devoted to British interests. My own belief, shared by many who were in the best position for judging at the time, is that during the crisis of the Rebellion, *before Delhi was taken*, the Native troops at Nagpore and Hyderabad were tampered with, and that such answers were returned to these overtures as clearly proved that the sympathies of the Madras Sepoys were entirely with the insurrectionary movement, and that if they had got a tempting opportunity they would have joined in it. They only wanted a beginning to be made, and a rallying-point of some sort,—the standard of a Prince, a popular pretender, or noted religious teacher, to be exhibited,—for them to take their part against us. No

* And the dispersion of which is said to be one object of the large force now assembled (October 1868) in the Hazara country under General Wilde.

such rallying-point appeared. No influential leaders came forward. The tentative outbreaks at Hyderabad and Nagpore failed; and after such a check to the first ebullition, it of course became doubly difficult to get the steam up again without some fresh encouragement. Instead of that, the tide turned steadily in favour of the British Government. Several plots and risings in the Mahratta Provinces, within the range and hearing, as may be said, of the Madras Army, failed signally. The conspiracy at Sattara was defeated and punished. The mutiny of Bombay troops at Kolapore was put down by General Le Grand Jacob in August; and a second attempted outbreak at the same place, in December 1857, was promptly crushed by the same officer, who had been invested by Lord Elphinstone with full civil and military powers. Delhi was taken in September; Lucknow was relieved in October 1857. British troops were beginning to disembark at every port. The moment of imminent danger passed away. But it would be a great mistake to underrate the magnitude and peril of the crisis that was safely passed through at Hyderabad and at Nagpore. At Hyderabad, the firmness and vigilance of Salar Jung, the Minister of the Nizam, with difficulty prevented a general Mahomedan rising. At Nagpore there were plottings enough, but owing to the wisdom and prudence of a venerable lady, the Banka Baee, (the widow of Rughojee the Second, who fought against us at Assaye and Argaum,) the most important conspiracy was never brought to maturity. The Mahratta Chieftains and old military officers of the Rajah at Nagpore, without her countenance would not attempt a rising; and the actual conspiracy, revealed and frustrated at the eleventh hour, was almost entirely carried on by Mussulman fanatics. As it was, their first blow very nearly succeeded. A little more encouragement from any member of the dethroned family, a little more boldness and determination, an hour or two more to perfect their preparations, would almost certainly have given immediate success to the Mahomedan conspirators. It is ten miles from the city of Nagpore to the military cantonment of Kamptee, where the small force of European troops was stationed. There was nothing to oppose the plan of murdering the Commissioner and his English assistants, and plundering the Treasury and Arsenal, which were then isolated and almost defenceless. A sufficient number of the local troops had joined in the plot, to have effected all this with ease, if they had acted promptly. Such an auspicious beginning would, in the month of June 1857, have terribly tried and shaken the Madras Sepoys; and the effect of the news on the immense and turbulent population of Hyderabad would probably have been decisive. An attack was made on the Hyderabad Residency by a body of insurgents on July 17th, 1857, which though feebly sustained, for want of an influential leader, shows the spirit that was abroad, and which a very little success would have rendered quite ungovernable. The Nizam and his Minister, Salar Jung, if they had endeavoured to stem the flood, would have been swept away, and some other member of the family raised to the throne. The Mahrattas of Poonah and Sattara, then hot-beds of conspiracy, and of Kolapore,—where both mutiny and rebellion subsequently occurred,—all the petty Rajahs and Sirdars of the South and West, would have risen at the signal from Nagpore. Kurnool and Cuddapah, two Madras districts containing numbers of warlike Pathan Mahomedans, would have followed the example of Hyderabad. And if the contagion of mutiny had once reached the Madras Sepoys,— especially through the medium of the Nizam, the Prince whom their leading men look up to,—it would have spread among them like wildfire, just as it did in the Bengal Army. Had one Madras Brigade gone wrong in the midst of the Delhi excitement, there would have been a series of disasters and massacres throughout the length and breadth of the Southern Presidency, then almost denuded of European troops. We should have had to make a fresh start from our stronghold at Calcutta or Bombay. Our enemies would have had time and space to organise and establish themselves as a regular Government, and no Native State could have continued to uphold our cause. We should no longer have been able to talk about a rebellion. We should have had to enter upon the conquest of India almost as foreign invaders, and without possession of the revenues.

From this incalculable aggravation of the horrors and perils of 1857, we were "saved," in the words of one of Lord Dalhousie's most constant and devoted admirers, "by the Nizam."* That Prince, the head of a State for sixty years in close and faithful alliance with us, had been told by Lord Dalhousie, in time of profound peace, and without consulting the Resident, that ours was "a great Government, whose power" could " crush him at its will,"† —a piece of vulgar blustering, which alone is sufficient to stamp the man who could make use of it as unfit for his exalted and dignified position. In the same letter Lord Dalhousie calls upon the Nizam, "to recognise the real dangers which surround" him.‡ How little did this arrogant adviser know where the real danger was to be looked for, and whom it threatened!

This menace of "crushing" seems to have been one of Lord Dalhousie's favourite formulas : he appears to have considered its application to our most faithful and submissive Allies peculiarly appropriate and impressive. We meet with these very words,—the bad taste heightened by bad grammar,—in the seventh paragraph of his Farewell Minute, applied to the present Rajah Runbeer Sing of Cashmere, son of Goolab Sing, who was then in a declining state of health :

"And when, as must soon be, the Maharajah shall pass away, his son, Meean Runbeer Sing, will have enough to do to maintain his ground against rivals of his own blood, without giving any cause of offence to a powerful neighbour, which he well knows can *crush him at his will.*"§

In July 1857, Rajah Goolab Sing did pass away, and Runbeer Sing, instead of wasting his resources in fighting any rivals, managed somehow or other to advance fifty

* " Madras was saved by the Nizam,"—*The Spectator*, October 6th, 1866,—see *Retrospects and Prospects of Indian Policy*, p. 203.
† *Papers, the Nizam*, 1854, p. 42. These words, taken from the official English version, are bad enough ; but the literal meaning of the Persian verb, '*paemal kardan*,' actually used in the Governor-General's letter, is '*to trample under foot.*' For this aggravation of the insult Lord Dalhousie cannot be held accountable, but it shows gross incompetence in the Persian Department of the Foreign Secretariat.
‡ *Papers, the Nizam*, 1854, p. 43.
§ *Marquis of Dalhousie's Minute*, 1856, p. 6.

lakhs of rupees (£500,000) to Sir John Lawrence, and to send 3,500 of his own troops to assist in the siege of Delhi.

At Hyderabad also, in the same critical period, the usual agitation and disorder of a succession occurred—Nasir-ood-Dowlah, the late Nizam, having died in July, 1857—yet the firmness of the present Prince restrained the warlike tribes and fanatical Mahomedans of his dominions and of Southern India, and facilitated every movement of the Madras Army; while more than one-half of that Hyderabad Contingent, which Lord Dalhousie politely informed the Nizam's father, in the letter already quoted, was "the main support on which depended the stability of his throne,"* was pushed forward beyond the Nizam's frontiers into our own provinces, to uphold the stability of *our* Empire against our own mutinous troops and our own rebellious subjects.

Yet from respect for the memory of such a false prophet as Lord Dalhousie, and to save the credit of such inconsiderable statesmen as Lord Lyveden and Lord Harris, this manifest iniquity, this reproach to the British Crown, and constant source of irritation and disgust to a most deserving, intelligent and industrious population, is to be confirmed and perpetuated! It is incredible. It cannot be. No one likes it; everyone is ashamed of it. Even Mr. Lowe, after having given his own version of the course of our relations with the Wallajah family, down to the rejection of Prince Azeem Jah, concluded by admitting that "he did not say that such transactions as these were matters which anyone could look at with great pleasure."†

No one has looked at them with any pleasure, since Lord Dalhousie's short-lived reputation was shivered to atoms in the earthquake of 1857. Not one Governor of Madras since Lord Harris, not one Indian Minister since Lord Lyveden, has reviewed the case of Prince Azeem Jah without evident compunction. The thing is notorious; it is patent to the world. Every Minute, every despatch that has seen the light, has tended to disclose the fact. Each successive debate in Parliament has presented the

* *Papers, the Nizam*, 1854, p. 41.
† *Hansard*, vol. clxxv, p. 1668.

spectacle of some leading statesman, in or out of office, eager to disclaim responsibility for this crying injustice. Sir Charles Wood tries in vain to shake it from his skirts. Lord Stanley plainly indicates that he would have redressed it if he had had time.*

The Chairman of the East India Company denies that there was anything like unanimity in the Court of Directors. Being taunted with having signed the despatch confirming the decision of Lords Harris and Dalhousie, Colonel Sykes, M.P. for Aberdeen, after strongly supporting the claims of Prince Azeem Jah in the debate of the 13th of July, 1864, observed that "the despatches were signed ministerially by the Directors, and that the opinions he entertained, when he signed that letter, were the same as he had now expressed."†

In short, the actual position of the British Government with reference to the Wallajah family rests on no authority at all. It has no moral basis; it is repudiated by the moral sense of every one who has examined it closely, even of those official persons who feel most acutely the formal difficulty of reversing it.

If, in order to apply another test, we even suppose the exclusion of Prince Azeem Jah from his father's dignity to be strictly just, no one can deny that the same injurious effect has been produced on the public mind as if it were grossly unjust. For this thing was not done in a corner. The machinery employed in executing and sustaining the Carnatic confiscation has been completely uncovered, and displayed to the whole world.

The working of British institutions is much more clearly understood and appreciated now-a-days in India, than was the case twenty years ago. Newspapers and Bluebooks are not only read by Natives of English education,

* Having voted for Mr. Smollett's motion in favour of Prince Azeem Jah on June 13th, 1864, in the conversation which followed the division Lord Stanley said that—"No decision was come to by him, as Secretary of State, on this subject. The memorial, no doubt, arrived when he was at the India Office; but, to the best of his recollection, he required further information about it, and therefore had no opportunity of coming to a decision on it before he quitted office."

† *Hansard*, vol. clxxv, p. 1667.

but are also transmitted and translated to the dependent Sovereigns, Chieftains and landlords. The names of our leading statesmen and their avowed or supposed views on Indian subjects, are known and canvassed in the Durbar and the closet of every Nawab and Rajah, and by all Natives who are interested in such matters throughout India. And in all classes, except the very lowest and most ignorant, there are many who are deeply interested.

Lord Canning did not fail to observe the momentous consequences that might ensue from the increasing publicity given to all the proceedings of our Government, and the growing avidity with which they were perused in India. His testimony is worthy of notice.

"Since 1849, the official correspondence on not less than sixteen or seventeen cases of doubtful succession and of adoption have been printed by orders of Parliament. In these papers there is every variety of opinion as to the claims of Native States on the one hand, and as to the duty, rights, and policy of the British Government on the other.

"And it must not be supposed that because these documents are published in Blue Books and in English they are beyond the knowledge of Native Courts. They are, on the contrary, sought for and studied by those whose dearest prospects they so closely affect. It is not many months since I was informed, by the Governor General's Agent in Central India, that a Native Court had received from England the Parliamentary Papers on Dhar before they had reached my own hand."*

Is there anything in the original process against Prince Azeem Jah, or in the course of his appeal, as placed before the world in the published documents and in the Parliamentary Debates, likely to persuade any person interested or any disinterested inquirer, I will not say that the Prince was justly excluded from the succession, but that any one can now believe him to have been justly excluded?

Of the Minutes and despatches it is unnecessary to say much more here. They have already been treated at sufficient length. From somewhat extensive personal inquiry, I can confidently assert that an intelligent Hindoo or Mussulman finds it so difficult fully to realise the insular arrogance which too often darkens the judgment and

* *Adoption Despatch* of April 30th, 1860, para. 7.

deadens the sympathies of British rulers in India, that statements and arguments which we simply set down as erroneous, appear to them so unfounded, unnatural and unreasonable, as to be quite irreconcilable with sincerity and good faith. They call them prevarications and subterfuges. I am afraid the judgment of an intelligent foreigner would be very much the same.

In 1854, when Nagpore was about to be annexed, Mr. Mansel, the Resident, hinted this very plainly to the Governor-General; but, of course, his words were wasted. "The reasons," he said, "for our refusal to allow adoption are *not intelligible* to the native aristocracy."*

However effective those statements and arguments may have been in the secret chambers of Madras and Leadenhall Street,—however conscientiously they may have been advanced, before the other side of the question was heard at all,—they have now been exposed to the light of day, to the rude air of public discussion, and will bear no more handling. Sir Charles Wood, in 1862, is seen to decline repeating them on his own authority. He gives a summary of them as "the grounds of the decision" of 1855, which he does not feel "justified in disturbing,"† but that is all.

Those who are inclined to favour Prince Azeem Jah's pretensions will hardly be convinced of their imaginary nature, when they see them supported by ninety-two members in an assembly always averse to such topics, and without the stimulus of a party struggle,—when they see the ungrateful task of bringing the subject before the House of Commons, undertaken by men of such divergent views in politics as Mr. Smollett, Mr. Layard and Mr. H. J. Baillie, repeatedly sustained by the chivalrous efforts of the present Lord Chief Baron, Sir Fitzroy Kelly, and sanctioned by a statesman so distinguished as Lord Stanley, who has been Secretary of State for India. Lord Stanley voted on the 13th of June, 1864, for Mr. Smollett's motion, and it was formally announced in the *Morning Herald* that he was only prevented by illness from voting for Sir Fitzroy Kelly's motion on the 14th of March 1865.

* *Further Papers, Berar*, 1856, p. 6.
† *Ante*, p. 81; Appendix A.

Never having been made a question of party, the case may be said never to have been fairly taken into consideration by the House of Commons. On the 13th of June, 1864, the Ministers, as already remarked, remained silent, and the debate was abruptly cut short by a division which was stigmatised as "a dodge." Ninety-two members voted or paired on the 14th of March, 1865, in favour of inquiry into the case, and the Government only obtained a majority of 15 by their own 24 official votes.

The Government cannot venture to subject their own proceedings to the calm consideration and report of a Select Committee, or even to make known the advice of their own law officers.

The formal support of the House of Commons can add no moral weight to the Government, while it refuses inquiry and avoids discussion, and yet escapes defeat at the hands of nearly a hundred independent members only by summoning its full official strength to vote in favour of its own decision. Including all the divisions, more than a hundred and twenty members have declared themselves in favour of Prince Azeem Jah's claims.

Three eminent Judges now on the bench, the Lord Chief Baron, Mr. Justice Lush and Sir Travers Twiss, and the present Advocate General of Madras, the Hon. J. B. Norton, the first-mentioned speaking many times from his place in Parliament, the others in written opinions,—have pronounced themselves convinced, without doubt or hesitation on any one point, of the justice of Prince Azeem Jah's pretensions, and of the utter groundlessness of the pretexts by which they have been hitherto disputed. All these opinions have been printed and published, and, like the debates and divisions in Parliament, are as well understood by those interested, and by educated Natives in India, as they are by us in England. What has the Government to set against them? The Minutes of Lord Harris, and the tacit approval of Lord Lyveden!

It is to be feared that the Government has trusted for the preservation of its moral and intellectual supremacy in India, in the face of such an array of indignant remonstrance, less to the world-wide fame and vast influence of the great authorities just mentioned, than to the political ignorance and apathy of the Indian people. That contemptuous policy may be pursued too far. Too much reliance may be placed on the apparent apathy of a people not encouraged or accustomed to tell us their feelings. The ignorance, also, may be less than we suppose. And after all, what *safety* is there in popular ignorance? Judging from historical experience, we should rather look upon it as a constant danger, most effectually tempered and restrained by extreme veneration for the persons and pageantry of hereditary Princes.

I trust I shall not be misinterpreted, or misunderstood, from anything I have said in the preceding section, as advising that the Nawab of the Carnatic should be reinstated, in order to conciliate the Southern Mahomedans, and avert their fanatical hostility, or in order to prevent a mutiny in the Madras Army. I do not profess to see any immediate cause for anxiety.

I am not one of those who believe in blood-thirsty fanaticism as an ordinary characteristic of the Mussulman faith.* I no more believe the Rebellion of 1857 to have been the result of a Mussulman plot, than I believe it to have been a mere military mutiny.

I am, in fact, much less of an alarmist than many of the most distinguished public servants, now actively employed in India. For example, Sir Richard Temple, then Resident at Hyderabad, in a despatch of the 16th August, 1867, from which I shall have to quote several passages of a more agreeable nature, writes as follows:—

* An able writer with whom I seldom have the good luck to agree, in an article of the *Edinburgh Review* for October 1866, on which I have made some comments elsewhere, (*Retrospects and Prospects of Indian Policy*, pp. 227, 235) has collected with great care some interesting facts recalling the large amount of aid afforded by Mussulman Princes, and the many instances of fidelity and devotion among Mussulman officials, during the terrible days of 1857.

"Not to go too far back, I have known, even within the last five peaceful years, instances occurring, on the average about once every two or three months, of seditious or treasonable productions, in all probability emanating from, or traceable to, the Brahmin priesthood. This hostility is even stronger in the Mahomedan priesthood; with them it literally burns with an undying flame; from what I know of Delhi in 1857-58, from what I am authentically informed of in respect to Hyderabad at that time, I believe that not more fiercely does the tiger hunger for his prey than does the Mussulman fanatic throughout India thirst for the blood of the white infidel. All this may be very sad, but it is no use disguising a fact which is inevitable."*

Nor do I look with suspicion upon the troops recruited from any province or district in India, or regard the Native Army as a necessary evil, to be kept at the minimum of numbers, and not to be trusted with the most efficient arms. If the Empire were organised so as to subserve the national honour and interests of both East and West, and not the professional interests and nepotism of the West only,—if the policy of contempt were abandoned, and a policy of confidence adopted,—India would become a source of military strength to Great Britain, instead of paralysing her right arm in peace, exposing incessantly a vulnerable point, where in war a well aimed blow might cause a fatal hemorrhage. There need be no distrust of Mahomedans, Sikhs, Poorbeeas, or Mahrattas, so long as the prevailing tone and temper of the country are in favour of the British Government, or at least in favour of order and obedience. So long as the leaders of the people are well disposed, the Army will be well disposed. If the Mussulman Chieftains and nobles are well disposed, the fanatics of that creed may be disregarded.

But we have done a great deal to make the leaders ill-disposed, while they have had much reason to feel their own value and their own strength, and to calculate ours,—which, enormous as it is, and is known by them to be, was before 1857 an incalculable mystery. The classes immediately below them,—and for several grades downwards,—among whom their instructors and advisers are to be found,—the reflective, active-minded classes, whether

* *British and Native Administration*, p. 71.

educated in the English or the Oriental style, are becoming daily more ambitious, more sensitive, more observant of the outer world, and of the political events and changes that are taking place elsewhere. As Sir Richard Temple recently remarked in the despatch to which I have already referred:—"In the event of any future European war or complication seriously involving Great Britain, we must be prepared for the people of India having a far nicer appreciation of the crisis than they have ever before had on similar occasions."* The masses, who obey no impulse that does not come from those of their own blood and language to whom they are accustomed to look up for guidance, are certainly not becoming more content with our rule. When most prosperous, they have no enthusiasm in its favour. In the words of Colonel W. F. Eden, Governor-General's Agent in Rajpootana, written in August, 1867,—"A Native administration has to a Native a warmth and geniality, if such terms may be applied, as compared with our Government, which, although admitted to be more just and equitable in all respects, strikes him as cold, hard, and unimpassioned."† But somehow or other, the people at large do not believe themselves to be prosperous under our rule. This is fully admitted by some of the ablest officers now engaged in the Government of British Provinces. Here is the opinion of Mr. R. H. Davies, Chief Commissioner of Oude, dated 16th July, 1867.

"An uneasy sense is felt of an intenser struggle more scantily rewarded. This, I am told by observant Natives, is the spreading sentiment among the rural classes. The complaint is that there is no *burkut* "(blessing)" under the British Government. It may be remembered that Colonel Sleeman mentions exactly the same grievance being adduced by the Jats of the Delhi territory. The meaning is that the toil is greater, nature more niggardly, the battle of life harder. The agrarian mind attributes the change to the foreign rule, to the remittance of money to England, to the decay of Native manufactures, to anything in short which runs counter to its prejudices."‡

* *Papers, British and Native Administration*, p. 74.
† *Ibid.*, p. 91.   ‡ *Ibid.*, p. 11.

A very similar account is given by the lamented Mr. A. A. Roberts, then Judicial Commissioner in the Punjaub, who died within a few months of the date of his letter, August 29th, 1867.*

Neither of these well-qualified witnesses rejects with scorn the notion that the people at large have any real grounds of discontent,—on the contrary, they rather support it. But it matters not for our present inquiry whether the popular complaints against the British Government are true or untrue, fair or unfair, reasonable or unreasonable. All that concerns us is that this uneasy, dissatisfied feeling exists, and is confined to no one class in particular. It indicates a loss of moral authority on the part of our Government. When that uneasy feeling has reached a certain pitch, and has lasted a certain time, the ruling Power, whatever it may be, ceases imperceptibly to lead or to govern the country,—it can only coerce. And when a Government is compelled to trust to physical power only, order may be preserved for a time, but there will be no real progress—none, at least, in favour of the governing class, or under its direction. A change may be slowly preparing, but when it comes it will be violent and destructive.

If we are once more to amass that great fund of moral power which Lord Dalhousie squandered, we must strike out a different course from that which has been pursued by his favourite Lieutenant for the last five years. The conservative elements which saved the Indian Empire from dissolution in its first great trial of 1857, have not been strengthened during the administration of Sir John Lawrence. On the contrary, they have been weakened and diluted. They have not, however, as yet been irretrievably scattered and wasted. It is doubtful whether, as they stand at present, they would operate as effectually in our favour, in the event of a second trial, as they did in the first. Nor must we expect a second trial to be exactly like the first.

The Bengal Sepoys would never have mutinied, if they had not fully expected, and with good reason, that they were only giving the signal for a general rising. Their

* *Papers, British and Native Administration*, p. 112.

reasoning was good, but insufficient. Statesmanlike observation and superior knowledge, fortified by the gallant bearing and unceasing instructions of the British Residents, kept the more considerable Native Sovereigns and their Ministers in the right path.* The minor Chieftains, restrained by their heavy stake from prematurely committing themselves, watched the movements of their more powerful brethren, and waited for something decisive. The attempt to re-establish the Imperial throne at Delhi, which appeared at the first blush to have been a politic step on the part of the mutineers, and a formidable blow to British power, was, in truth, the turning point in our favour. It frightened the Hindoo Princes, and threw the Sikhs into our arms. But while it frightened the Princes, to whom it suggested territorial restitution, tribute, and vassalage, it pleased their soldiers and subjects, and roused the leading spirits among them to enthusiasm. And thus we saw Scindia and Holkar, the two most important

* The only Resident at a Native Court of any consequence who broke down completely in the crisis of 1857, was Colonel (now Sir Henry) Durand, in charge of the Residency at Indore, Holkar's capital, during the absence of Sir Robert Hamilton. He was so blind to what was passing close to his own doors, so neglectful of friendly intercourse with the Court and its notabilities, so arrogantly regardless of Native counsels and opinions, that an attack upon his own house by the insurgent party took him quite by surprise, and forced him to leave the place, escorted by some faithful troopers in the service of the Begum of Bhopal, and to take refuge in the British station of Hoshungabad. Here he rushed into the opposite extreme,—jumped to the conclusion that the Maharajah Holkar was implicated in the revolt, and declared, in the style of Napoleon, "The dynasty of Holkar has ceased to reign!" Fortunately Sir Robert Hamilton returned from England towards the close of 1857, and his great personal influence and local knowledge supplied what was wanting, while Colonel Durand, now in his true element as a Brigadier General, was doing good service in the field. The long list of errors committed by this respectable officer during fifteen years employment in civil and diplomatic duties,—always arising from the same hard sectarian prejudices, always evincing the same inability to estimate human character, and to measure human motives,—being apparently counterbalanced by his industry, business talents, and distinguished military services, he has since that time held the high offices of Foreign Secretary to Government and Member of the Viceroy's Council, during which period his persistent efforts to confiscate Dhar and annex Mysore, barely failed. Yet he is still probably considered a high authority by some people.

Princes of Central India, thrown into antagonism with a strong body of their own relatives, troops, and followers, and their authority far a time overpowered by a vehement party of action. The news of the House of Timour having resumed Imperial sway raised an excitement and spread temptations abroad, that nothing could resist but the weighty personal responsibility, the fixed personal interests, and the limited personal ambition of a reigning Sovereign. But for this, every barrier would have been broken, there would have been no rallying point for the prudent and orderly, no place of refuge and repentance for those who found out their mistake in time.

The spectacle of Hindoos and Mussulmans cordially uniting to hail the visionary revival of their ancient Monarchy, should have suggested to any Indian statesman worthy of the name, that for the future we must only count to a very slight extent upon religious animosity and rivalry preventing political combinations in India. Our own practice and our own example,—the liberties and the disabilities, the merits and demerits of our rule,— following hard upon the discipline and policy of Mahratta state-craft, have gone very far to extinguish the jealousies of race and creed, to place all tribes on an equal footing, and to foster the germs of a national feeling. There is nothing now between us and the masses, but their Princes. And the Princes, if we do not spurn them, are entirely subject to our influence. We may continue to administer our Provinces in quiet times, but we cannot govern India without the aid of its natural leaders.

What has been the course of the Indian Government since these lessons were offered for its learning? Everything that it ought not to have been. Lord Canning caught a glimpse of the light, but not enough to guide him towards a complete and consistent policy. With a brief interval in the last two years of his administration, marked by the Adoption Despatch, and the restoration of two districts to the Nizam, there has been no change in the aspect of the Calcutta Foreign Office towards the dependent Princes; and during the incumbency of Sir John Lawrence, it has drifted back altogether into the old ways. Though advantage has very properly been taken of a turbulent Regency to assume the management of Bhawulpoor, there is no visible sign or symptom of any general or definite plan for reforming the Native States, or for harmonising their institutions to some extent with those of our own Provinces. Not only has there been no measure of restitution, but every possible effort was made to annex Mysore; and although Mr. Bowring, the Commissioner in charge of that State, has shown himself quite ready and willing to carry out the intentions of Her Majesty's Government, every possible obstacle is now employed to postpone the installation or public recognition of the young Maharajah, and to prevent or delay the substitution of Native for English management during his minority.*

The able official of a stiff and narrow school, who, by an experiment not likely to be repeated, has been left for five years in a place that demands a real statesman, seems to have had only one idea for making British supremacy felt among the dependent Principalities, and that was by making it extremely disagreeable. At the great Durbar held in Agra, in November, 1866, he lectured and scolded the assembled Princes in the very style that was best calculated to offend and disgust, and to determine them never again to expose themselves willingly to such public humiliation.† When he met the Punjaub Chieftains at Lahore, there was nothing noticeable in his addresses, except some self-complacent references to his own career in that Province, and a glorification of those British rulers of India who could speak the vernacular dialects.‡

But this mere want of tact and taste, this bad style in matters of Imperial representation,—though a serious

---

* We have just heard that the young Rajah was enthroned on the 23rd September, 1868, but as this was done in pursuance of peremptory orders from the Secretary of State, nothing in the text requires alteration.

† See the *Pall Mall Gazette* of the 24th December, 1866.

‡ A knowledge of Hindustani, or any other language spoken in India, is likely to be about as useful to a Viceroy or Governor, as a knowledge of Russian or Spanish would be to our Prime Minister,— an accomplishment not to be despised, but no qualification.

deficiency in a Viceroy,—is not the smallest fault with which Sir John Lawrence's rule is to be charged. In the general demeanour of his Government towards the Native States, and in several recent measures affecting them, which bear the stamp of his individuality, there has been a marked professional tone, a nasty twang of the old Collector. The rulers of millions, connected with the Paramount Power by Treaties of perpetual friendship and alliance, have been addressed and treated in a departmental manner, as if they really were what the *Friend of India* and other official organs rejoice to call them, "feudal nobles," as if their dominions were their "estates," and their subjects were their "tenants." For instance, something very like a graduated scale of fines was instituted, to be imposed on Native States on the occurrence of any robbery of our mail in its transit through the dominions of our Allies. We may remark, by the bye, that such robberies, and robberies of all sorts, are notoriously quite as frequent in our territories as in theirs.

It has just been remarked, that in the crisis of 1857, the two most important Sovereigns of Central India, the Rajahs Scindia and Holkar, found their personal influence insufficient for a time to restrain a large party of their troops and followers from joining in the Rebellion. The chief obstacle to the free exercise of the Maharajah Scindia's authority in the worst days of the Rebellion, the chief support of the turbulent party around him, consisted of the Gwalior Contingent, a force complete in itself,—Horse, Foot, and Artillery,—with its own arsenal, stores, and cash-chest, raised and disciplined by British officers, according to what used to be considered the only *safe* plan for organising Native troops. The expense of this force was imposed upon the Gwalior State by Treaty, when its unmanageably large Army had been disbanded after Lord Ellenborough's campaign of 1843. At a very early period of the outbreak, the Gwalior Contingent mutinied, some of the English officers being murdered. The mutineers, nearly ten thousand strong, of all arms, left their cantonments, preserving their military order under chosen leaders, and thronged, clamorous and wild with excitement, around the Maharajah Scindia's Palace, calling on him to lead them to Delhi. How the brave young Prince confronted this formidable host, how he humoured them, and temporised with them, since he could not fight them,—though he tried that also at last, and failed; how he kept them idle and harmless for months at Gwalior, until Delhi was taken, and how, after marching on Cawnpore and holding General Windham at bay, the mutineers of the Gwalior Contingent, still a compact body, were at last routed by Lord Clyde, are matters of history, and need not be described here at full length. What concerns us at present, is, that on the establishment of order, the Gwalior Contingent having been wiped out, its several posts and military duties were taken up by regular British troops, and by the Maharajah's augmented forces. As the Contingent system had manifestly failed in this instance, a new treaty was concluded, ratified by Lord Canning on the 12th December, 1860, under which, certain pecuniary advantages were conferred on the Gwalior State, and its military force, restricted under the Treaty of 1844, might be raised to the limit of "5000 drilled" (Infantry) "soldiers, 6000 Sowars," (troopers) and "36 guns with 360 gunners."*

Events had shown, that, but for the contagion of our revolted Sepoys, the Maharajah Scindia could have easily kept his own people quiet.† At an advanced stage of the Rebellion, his own troops, though quite as ill disposed towards us as our mutineers, were in a great measure obedient to the Maharajah's commands, so far at least as to be inactive and innocuous: while the men of the Gwalior Contingent, brought up under British discipline, from which they had broken loose, set him at defiance,

* Article ix of the Treaty of 1860; *Collection of Treaties*, Calcutta, 1864 (London, Longmans,) vol. iv, p. 274.

† Holkar, who had in some respects less difficulties to contend with than Scindia, and got over them more quickly, would doubtless have played as good a game on our side, and have won as much renown as his neighbour, if he had been equally fortunate in having at his Court such a friend and adviser as Major Samuel Charters Macpherson, the Resident at Gwalior, Scindia's capital. But it was not so; and consequently Holkar was under a cloud for some time; his services were hardly appreciated and poorly requited.

and took the field against us. As there was no doubt or question of the loyalty and steadfastness of this excellent Prince, which had been tried severely enough,—Scindia having perilled his life in our cause with conspicuous gallantry on several occasions,—one would have supposed that the wisest and most natural policy would have been by every possible means to increase his influence, and strengthen his hands within his own dominions. And such, in fact, was Lord Canning's policy, which Sir John Lawrence has done his best to shake to pieces,—as in like manner, and from the same professional habits and prejudices, he perseveringly tried to upset Lord Canning's policy in Oude, with regard to the Talookdars, and the tenure of land in their estates.

Scindia, who is described as being a born soldier, with a remarkable talent for military organisation and evolutions, well pleased with the concessions of the Treaty of 1860, had taken full advantage of them to indulge his martial tastes. The greater part of his little army, the "*drilled soldiers*" permitted by the new Treaty, were massed at his capital under his own eye; and here, in unsuspecting complacency, about two years ago,[*] he invited the British Resident to witness a grand review of all his troops. Whether the Resident or the Viceroy first took fright, I do not know, but the immediate result was an absolute order, in some form or other, from the Government of India to the Maharajah, desiring that his little Army should at once be broken up, the several corps dispersed about the country, and that no such large assemblage of troops should again take place.

It would be difficult to conceive a measure more miserable and more unmeaning. I might urge that such peremptory interference is inconsistent with the engagements between the British Government and that of Scindia. The Treaty of 1860, which limits the number of troops, permits no control over their location or distribu-

---

[*] I have mislaid my memorandum of the date and particulars of this transaction, as described in the Indian papers, but as they were unanimous in praising the action of Government there can be little doubt as to the facts, though I trust for them to my memory.

tion; while, in Article VIII of the Treaty of 1804, confirmed by every subsequent engagement, it is expressly stipulated that "no officer of the Honourable Company shall ever interfere in the internal affairs of the Maharajah's Government;"* and Article IV of the Treaty of 1817, confirmed and declared to be "binding" in the Treaty of 1860, pronounces the Maharajah to be "the undisputed master of his own troops and resources."† No stress need be laid upon these conditions; they are only to be taken as a starting-point; for undoubtedly, the Paramount Power, responsible for the peace of the Empire, cannot be bound by the strict letter of Treaties, when the public safety is endangered, and immediate action may be required to check hostile intrigue or dangerous excitement. Nor is any account or explanation of suspicions and precautions due to the minor State. But such coercive action, equivalent to open war against a Power of equal standing, ought to be very sparingly used, and only in case of urgent necessity. Sir John Lawrence could allege no such necessity for interfering with Scindia's legitimate authority over his own troops, within his own territories. He manifested groundless mistrust of a subordinate Ally before all India. Nothing could have been more impolitic or more ungracious. It was just the old leaven of the permanent official, the characteristic disease of the Bengal Civilian,—a sort of fussy jealousy, always sure to be roused by the portentous phenomenon of any Native, whether Prince or peasant, displaying the slightest originality or independence, presuming to act or think for himself.

Even if there had been any cause or ground for mistrust, it was most indiscreet and undignified to show it. There could be no actual *danger* or *menace* to British supremacy in the encampment of our Ally's small Army,— a mere Division of second-rate Sepoys after all,—at his capital. The idea is ridiculous. What ought, therefore, to have been done under the circumstances, is obvious. On receiving the Resident's report of the unlooked for efficiency and smartness of Scindia's troops, a Viceroy who

* *Collection of Treaties*, vol. iv, p. 236.   † *Ibid.*, p. 272.

had any statesmanlike insight, would have grasped at once at the opportunity of raising the self-respect of a well-disposed Prince, and of promoting substantial and solid progress in one of the largest Native States. He would have congratulated and complimented the Maharajah on having commenced of his own accord the reform of his establishments by that of his Army, which he rejoiced to hear was now in a high state of discipline; and he would then have suggested some other public department, organised on a faulty principle, where improvements, hinted or sketched in outline, might be introduced with great advantage to the people, and with great honour to his Highness's name.

Even while these pages are printing, the following paragraph appears in the *Overland Times of India* of the 26th September, 1868, extracted from the Calcutta Journals:—

"The Government have issued orders directing that only a limited number of troops are to be maintained in Native States, and that only one year's ammunition is to be issued to such levies."

So that the orders issued to the Gwalior State were evidently no accidental or isolated manifestation of mistrust. They were issued in obedience to a great principle! Sir John Lawrence, Viceroy of India, considers it a proud and prudent policy to tell the Native States all round, that the Imperial Power is afraid of them, and declines their military services. Although a great number of these States pay no tribute whatever, the Governor-General insists on relieving them from all military expense or responsibility, and deliberately saddles the whole burden of the external and internal defence of the Empire upon the British Government for ever.

There may be differences of opinion as to the merits of this policy; but no one can deny that it is very unlike that which Lord Canning had designed and partially carried out during the last two years of his administration, and which is shadowed forth in the following remarkable passages of his last private letter to General Sir Mark Cubbon, dated the 24th November, 1860.

"I have no doubt that the policy of disruption and separation was the right one fifty years ago, when the Rohillas and Mahrattas possessed armies and artillery which they could increase at pleasure without our consent, and, indeed, without our knowledge. But now it is quite different. These Chiefs can scarcely cast a gun,—they certainly could not equip it unknown to us. They feel their dependence on us, since 1857 more than ever. We have nothing to fear from them individually, if we treat them rightly; whilst they have individually an influence which is invaluable to us as Supreme Rulers in India, if we will but turn it to account. To do this, we must put them in a position to become useful instruments of civil government, and to take a pride in it. It is not a hopeless task, as some pretend. If it were, Scindia would not, in May last, when I was returning to Calcutta, have taken his place in the mail-cart, to meet me on the Trunk Road, for no other purpose than to show me the results of his own revision of his revenue assessments, made in compliance with exhortations given to him six months before at Agra.

"In one way or another—in every way, in short—we must teach these men unmistakeably, that, whether they be Chiefs of States or subjects, no change of the Supreme Power in India will be a gain to them, either as regards property, religion, social position, or national prejudices; and that the largest possible share of consideration and authority which they can have under any Paramount Power, they shall have under ours. If, as is very probable, the day of a European war is not distant, the need to us of such a conviction in their minds will soon make itself felt. To hold our Indian Empire in its present dimensions, through a war with France and Russia, we must hold it by some other means than the few English Regiments which, in such a case, would be spared to us."*

The troops of dependent Sovereigns, so long as their pay, regularly disbursed, does not unduly encroach on the local finances, cannot be made too efficient. Native troops, properly organised, cannot be kept under any control equally effective with that of a Native Prince, whose personal and hereditary ties and engagements constitute a chain of subordination and responsibility to the Paramount Power, more clearly defined and more easily enforced than any that have ever yet existed, or can be devised.

* A longer extract from this admirable letter was printed in the Appendix to *Retrospects and Prospects of Indian Policy.*

It would be out of place here, and foreign to the matter in hand, were I to enter on the detailed negotiations and arrangements, by which, through some such favourable opening as Sir John Lawrence unhappily rejected and perverted, a Native Prince might be led to adopt cheerfully the path of order and reform; by which his troops might be associated and identified with ours, without his dignity or authority being lowered; by which all frontier customs or transit duties, impeding commerce between his Provinces and ours should be abolished; by which, perhaps, the process of our Courts might run in his dominions, and that of his in ours. The administrative and executive reform of a Native State is not a plant that can grow to its full size in a day. Tact and cordiality, genial confidence. and warm appreciation of small beginnings, may make the plant strike deep root. The cold shade and rough usage to which official cultivation has been of late confined, can only stunt the growth, corrupt the soil and poison the atmosphere.

In this matter of the Maharajah Scindia's Army, the action of Sir John Lawrence seems to have involved every fault that should be avoided in dealing with the dependent States. (1.) It betrayed petty suspicions and inglorious apprehensions, unworthy of the Imperial Power. (2.) It violated a Treaty,—thereby shaking respect for the solemn engagements on which the moral authority of our Government depends, not only in the particular State injured, but in every State throughout India. (3.) It tended to alienate an able and estimable Prince, and to make British supremacy hateful and offensive in his councils, and among all his compeers. (4.) By an affront so galling, and so publicly administered, aimed at what was known to be the Maharajah's special pride and tenderest point, his influence must have been weakened generally in his own dominions, and that of the malcontent and turbulent party everywhere enhanced. (5.) The influence of the Maharajah, faithfully and beneficially exerted on our side in the last great crisis, has been weakened exactly where, judging from the experience of those days, it most required strengthening,—his personal and undivided command over his own troops.

Having thus lowered at one stroke the moral power of Great Britain, and of a most useful and deserving friend, what positive result did Sir John Lawrence obtain? Nothing that I can see, except that of having made himself intensely disagreeable. He did not in the least diminish the physical force available for bad purposes within Scindia's territories. He weakened the Maharajah's controlling influence over it; he certainly gained none for any British authority. He probably offended and disgusted an intelligent and high-spirited Prince; he assuredly pleased nobody.

No—there I am not doing full justice to his "vigilant and vigorous policy." It did please somebody. It delighted the *Friend of India*. This Calcutta weekly paper, which lives on its official connection, and has been for many years more or less the organ of the local Government,* has never abandoned the rapacious doctrines of Lord Dalhousie's era, although, as we shall see, it has done what, according to its code of political morality, is a very different thing,—it has *forsworn* them. Bewildered a little, as were the official oracles from which it draws its inspiration, by the glare of the Rebellion, and still more by the gleam of sunshine in the last year of Lord Canning's administration, it soon recovered its wonted animation, and resumed its usual course of abusing, insulting and threatening the most powerful, faithful and influential of our friends.

The following passage from the *Friend of India*, of the 25th of October, 1860, has never perhaps been surpassed:—

"Annexation is in abeyance for the hour, and it is right that Government should forswear all approach to it now. But the destiny of British power is in time to sweep the effete Princelings who now rule Hyderabad, Gwalior, Indore, Guzerat, and Travancore off the face of the Peninsula."

* *Ante*, note, p. 74. See also many allusions in General Sir William Sleeman's letters, (*Sleeman's Oude*, vol. ii, p. 390, etc.) This journal has been occasionally edited, for short periods, by Government officials, and is frequently enriched by their contributions and communications.

We are to "*forswear*" for the present that policy which it is our "destiny" to accomplish "*in time,*" or as soon as possible. Forswear annexation: swear eternal friendship; swear to respect treaties "*for the hour,*" the pear is not ripe!

On the 7th March, 1861, the *Friend* talked of "weeding out the estates of such feudal nobles as Scindia and Holkar," in order "to arrive at simplicity of government and vigour of administration."

Of course, when such questions as the confiscation of Dhar, and, when that was averted, its retention under the management of an English officer long after the Prince had attained his majority, and the maintenance of Mysore as a Native State, were yet undecided, the Editor of the *Friend of India* upheld with might and main, both in his ordinary sphere and in his far more serviceable capacity as Correspondent of the *Times,* the views of the Calcutta Foreign Office, and burst into ecstasies of invective when those views were combated and finally negatived by the Home Government. A little damped under Lord Canning's later administration, all the old fire revived under that of Sir John Lawrence.

In his letter which appeared in the *Times* of 6th December, 1865, he denounced the Rajah of Mysore as "a tyrannical sensualist," and informed the readers of the leading journal that this Prince "*enjoyed an income greater than the whole Civil List of England.*" The Rajah's income was about £120,000 a-year. This writer blunders terribly whenever he touches on figures. He erroneously states that "*we*" "twice paid the debts" of the Rajah of Mysore. He reiterates this mistake several times, and in a letter which was published in the *Times* as late as the 24th August, 1868, he speaks of "the large sums *we* more than once gave" the Rajah of Mysore, "to pay his debts," asserting with a distinctness that convicts him, that "*the money*" issued "*for the repeated payment of the Maharajah's debts came directly out of the Indian Treasury.*" This is a very inaccurate statement. "We" never gave the Rajah a penny to pay his debts, or for any other purpose. No sum of money paid to him, or on his account, ever came out of "the Indian Treasury." His debts were paid from the accumulated surplus revenues of his own Kingdom, which amounted in 1861, when General Cubbon left Mysore, to upwards of a million sterling in hard cash, deposited in the Treasury at Bangalore. The Maharajah claimed this accumulated surplus. Into the strength of his demand, and the cogency of the argument by which it was supported, it is quite needless to enter. Our Government very properly declined to place this vast sum at his uncontrolled disposal; but practically admitted his predominant claim over the fund by paying his debts from it, investing the remainder in 4 per cent. paper, and remitting the annual interest from this investment for his Highness's private use.*

Such is the true state of the case with regard to the payment of the Rajah's debts; and if contrasted with the description given by the Editor of the *Friend of India*, some notion may be formed of the trustworthiness, even in a simple matter of account with which he was fully acquainted, of the irresponsible anonymous writer who in Calcutta has the credit of being the organ of Government House, and in London has the immense advantage of occupying the columns of the *Times*.

In his frantic efforts to make the prospective restoration of a Native Government in Mysore appear odious, this writer indulges in indiscriminate abuse of all Native Governments. In a letter to the *Times* dated the 10th of March, 1866, he declares that in Native States, "*mutilation, the ravishing of women, torture, suttee, and samadh, or burying alive, are the rule.*" In a letter dated March 9th, which appeared in the *Times* of the 8th April, 1867, he says that the restoration of Mysore would be "equivalent to the restoration of slavery in the West Indian Colonies," and that "*horrible oppression is inseparable from the rule of an idolatrous Hindoo or sensual Mussulman.*" "No education but Christian principle or a miracle," can, according to him, make the Mysore Rajah's heir fit to rule over his Hindoo countrymen. He deplores "Lord Cranborne's act"—which he subsequently terms

* *Mysore Papers*, 1866, (No. 112) pp. 42, 44.

"folly" and "political cowardice," and declares to have done "much to provoke a future rebellion,"—"in promising to make over the four millions of Mysore to a boy whose rule can never be made better than that of other Native Chiefs,—that is, will be as bad as the Bourbons of Naples or Spain."*

But he is not content with general objurgation. In order to give point and colour to his weekly articles, and to the paraphrase of them which each mail brings for our edification, he assiduously rakes together every scandalous tale, every rumour of violence, oppression or intrigue in Native Principalities, that he can pick up among the official underlings, the missionaries and the indigo planters of his acquaintance; and these he spreads abroad as established facts through the medium of the leading journal of Great Britain. Any complaint against a Native Prince or Minister that appears in a petition sent to the Calcutta Foreign Office, is at once set down as sufficiently well founded for his purpose. Any assertion or opinion of any British Agent, even the Palace gossip of a Resident's diary, is gospel truth for him, if it falls in with his ordinary strain, or, is "communicated" from the right quarter.

And thus during the last three or four years, the Sovereigns of nearly all the more considerable States, many of them excellent rulers, all of them exemplary as dependent Allies, have been exposed in turn to the insulting calumnies of the *Friend of India*, which receive a publicity and a weight denied to the utterances of any other Indian journal, by being repeated at short intervals in the columns of the *Times;* and in which each Native Court, arguing from past events and current report, seems to hear the first mutterings of some official storm, the advent of some coercive policy, the revival of schemes of annexation.

In his letter to the *Times*, dated the 10th of March,

---

* Was the Government of the Bourbons quite as bad as all that? Were "mutilation, the ravishing of women, torture, etc., the rule," in Spain and Naples? But no writer can always preserve exactly the same level of fine writing or of accuracy.

1866, protesting against any transfer of territory to Native rule that has ever been under British management, he draws a sad picture of the internal condition of the little State of Jheend. "Only in 1859," he says, "we gave some lands to the Sikh Rajah of Jheend, and to this day the sound of his artillery may be heard putting down the revolt of the oppressed peasantry."

One of the most gallant and faithful of our feudatories is shown up as a tyrant, in whose Principality a rebellion has raged—he speaks of no intermission,—for seven years, artillery being used against the insurgent peasantry. If this had really been going on in 1866, Sir John Lawrence ought to be called to account, and also Sir Robert Montgomery, who was then Lieutenant Governor of the Punjaub. But I suspect "the sound of that artillery" never reached their ears.

In the recently printed Blue Book on *British and Native Administration* compared, the present Lieutenant Governor of the Punjaub, Sir Donald Macleod, in a letter dated 5th September, 1867, refers in the following terms to the brotherhood of Sikh Chieftains under his immediate supervision, among whom the Rajah of Jheend holds a leading place :—

"The principal Cis-Sutlej Chiefs and the Rajah of Kuppoorthulla have made considerable progress of late years towards the adoption of more enlightened principles of government."*

If a rebellion, requiring artillery for its suppression, had been recently raging in Jheend, I think we should have heard something of it in these Papers. Another distinguished officer, Sir Richard Temple, for many years Sir John Lawrence's right-hand man in the Punjaub, now Finance Minister of India, in a despatch to be found in the same collection, mentions this very State of Jheend in terms far from condemnatory.

"From 1854 to 1860 I had particular knowledge of the protected Sikh States, Cis-Sutlej. These are intertwined and interlaced amongst British districts supposed to be administered in our very best method. Yet I never knew any immigration from

* *Papers, British and Native Administration*, 1868, p. 113.

those States to our districts. The villages of the Puttiala and *Jheend* States especially were among the finest and happiest I have ever known, and seemed to be on a par with the choicest pieces of British territory."

And I think I must add the two sentences immediately following.

"From 1863 to 1867 I have been acquainted with the British districts on the frontiers of the Native States of Bundelcund, of Scindia, and Bhopal; and have never observed that the people preferred our management over that of the Native States. Indeed several tracts in that quarter had been unsuccessfully managed by the British, though we may hope that this has of late years been retrieved."*

Another paragraph from the same despatch, though not actually necessary, or strictly relevant to my present purpose, may strengthen the corrective already given to the sweeping calumnies of the *Friend of India*.

"In 1864 I passed through the Baroda territory (the Gaekwar's Dominions); certainly that district, the valley of the Mhye, is in external prosperity hardly surpassed by any British district, any that I have ever seen at least. In the Deccan, of late years, the constitution, system, and principles of the Nizam's civil government are really excellent; this much is certain. That the result must be more or less beneficial to the country is hardly to be doubted. Whether full effect is given to the intentions of His Highness's Government, throughout the Deccan, I cannot yet say; but independent testimony is constantly reaching me to the effect of great improvement being perceptible. Judging from the published reports, I should suppose that the Native administration in Travancore must be excellent. I believe, too, that the administration of the Gwalior country, when under the Minister Dinkur Rao, afforded a fair example of what Native rule can accomplish, and that it still continues good under the Maharajah Scindia. I have, on the whole, a favourable opinion of the administration of the Nagpore country by the Mahratta Sovereigns of the Bhonsla House. There were many excellent points about their rule; but some of these were owing to the care of British Officers such as Sir R. Jenkins, Colonel Wilkinson, and others."†

Of improvements in Native administration so instituted and so maintained, we may well be proud, as also of the effects of our general influence described in the following

* *Papers, British and Native Administration*, 1868, p. 69.
† *Ibid.*, p. 69.

sentence of a despatch from Mr. J. H. Morris, Chief Commissioner of the Central Provinces, dated 23rd August, 1867.

"The administration of Bhopal, of Travancore, of Puttiala, of the Putwurdhuns, of Gwalior, would not be what it is, if it were not for the example, and influence of the Paramount Power. The influence of our Residents, the example of our government, the competition of our provinces, compel Native States to maintain order, to administer a sort of justice, to curb exaction."*

"Our own Correspondent" in the same letter of the 10th of March, 1866, goes on to draw another picture, equally false in effect, though with a sufficient groundwork of truth to save his formal veracity, as that last quoted about the "dread artillery" of Jheend.

"Political considerations have led us to make frequent exchanges of land with feudatories like Scindia and the Nizam, and more heart-rending cries than those which the tenantry have sent up to us I have never read."

These "heart-rending cries" were "read" by him, no doubt, in petitions forwarded to the Calcutta Foreign Office, during the first alarm of change. Let us hear the testimony of Sir Richard Temple, when Resident at Hyderabad, as to the actual results of the retransfer of the Raichore and Dharaseo districts, after six years of British administration, to the Nizam's Government.

"I certainly have understood, from officers in a position to know, that the people much regretted the retransfer, and were full of apprehension. Such, I believe, was the fact at the time, *though they have since not had any cause to lament, for the Nizam's civil government in that quarter has been well conducted.*"†

In the same letter the Calcutta Correspondent declares that "Lord Stanley's persistence in causing the restoration of Dhar *has reduced that State*" to "*a miserable condition.*" This is utterly untrue. It is, at best, a gross exaggeration, founded on some scrap from a despatch or petition which he was allowed to see at the Foreign Office. Dhar is going on very well.

* *Papers, British and Native Administration*, p. 85.
† *Ibid.*, p. 69.

In his letter from Calcutta of the 9th March, 1867, published in the *Times* of the 8th April, 1867, still harping on Mysore, he forgets "Lord Stanley's persistence in causing the restoration of Dhar," and says that "Lord Stanley should have checked his late colleague," (Lord Cranborne,) "for *he* knows well the evil involved in such an act, contrary to all our policy." Certainly contrary to "*our*" policy,—the policy during the last twenty years of the *Friend of India*, his official patrons and his familiar associates,—the clerks, the shopkeepers, the indigo planters and the missionaries, that mixed English and half-caste population, the colonial cockneydom of Calcutta. I doubt whether *their* policy, even if they dignify it by the name of Lord Dalhousie's, will ever be Lord Stanley's. Lord Dalhousie himself might have known better by this time, but the cockneydom of an official metropolis is not easily cured.

In this letter the writer drops all restraint, and having charged Lord Cranborne with "folly" and "political cowardice," displays his own political audacity by what is perhaps the grossest outrage upon which he has yet ventured. As an illustration of what he pretends to be the course of Native rule, he refers to that of Holkar, "who," according to him, "*mutilates his tenantry, carries off their wives*, and rackrents their holdings till they desert them."

In this case I doubt very much if he had even the smallest scrap of a despatch or petition as the germ of his crop of slanders. Here he had, at the most, some flying rumour to salve his very easy conscience under the guilt of bearing false witness against his neighbour. The Maharajah Holkar of Indore has always borne a high character for humanity and benevolence, and has shown many signs of being an enlightened ruler; and whatever defects there may be in his system of government, it is quite free from any stain of those horrors which are here recklessly imputed to the Prince himself in person.

Setting aside the specific atrocities imputed by the Correspondent, if Holkar's Government were very bad, we should expect that the inhabitants of a district about to be transferred from our administration to his, would look upon the approaching change with dread and dismay. On this point let us hear the testimony of Mr. J. H. Morris, Chief Commissioner of the Central Provinces, in a letter to the Government of India, dated the 23rd of August, 1867.

"There has been for some years an impending exchange of territory with Holkar, which will involve the transfer to the Indore Durbar of two or three Nimar Pergunnahs. So far as our officers can judge, the people of those tracts feel no dislike at the prospect of re-transfer to Native rule. Again, many of our Nerbutta Valley landholders also own villages in Bhopal or under the Gwalior Durbar; and they always speak with respect and contentment of the treatment they receive at the hands of the Revenue authorities there."*

It is true that the Blue Book from which I am now quoting, discloses a difference of opinion among experienced officials as to the indifference or satisfaction of the inhabitants of these tracts on the question of their change of masters;† but while the evidence of Mr. J. H. Morris, the officer within whose jurisdiction the Nimar Pergunnas were then actually included, is at least as weighty as any one else's, the opposing statements confirm my charge of slander against the Editor and Correspondent, for their strictures on Holkar's administration contain no hint or suggestion of cruelty or oppression, and amount merely to the usual assertion of the superiority of our system.

In this same letter which appeared in the *Times* of the 8th April, 1867, he describes the Hindoo Maharajah of Guzerat, whose capital is at Baroda, as "the Gaekwar, *who ties his enemies to the feet of an elephant to be trampled to death.*" Here he has got hold of a particle of truth, which he manipulates into a monstrous falsehood. The solitary instance of a great criminal having been executed at Baroda three years ago in a barbarous manner, after trial and condemnation, is employed by him so as to convey the impression that such events are of frequent

* *Papers, British and Native Administration*, 1868, p. 85.
† See page 96, where Colonel Meade, Governor-General's Agent for Central India, thinks that "the proposed transfer has caused a painful feeling among the people." See also p. 99 of the same Blue Book.

occurrence, that the Gaekwar summarily disposes of his personal "*enemies*" by this revolting process,* that the general course and aspect of his Government is ferocious and oppressive.

In the letter which appeared in the *Times* of the 27th October, 1868, he says that in the annual Reports of the Political Agents on the Native States to which they are attached, we "have the materials for a much more trustworthy judgment regarding the comparative merits of English and Asiatic rule than were afforded by the Correspondence on that subject published last year." The numerous extracts I have given from that Correspondence will explain his distaste for it. But let us take him at his word. Let us see whether the picture of the Gaekwar's Government drawn by the Resident at his Highness's Court, corresponds with the bold sketch presented by the Editor of the *Friend of India* to the readers of the *Times*, or with that given by Sir Richard Temple.† The Report on the administration of Baroda for the year 1867, by Colonel J. T. Barr, the Resident, is dated in March, 1868. I shall commence by quoting the most unfavourable passage I can find in it.

Occasionally, he says, he has received reports of "mismanagement on the part of the Durbar officials, causing loss of revenue, and sometimes injustice to portions of the population, not, however, amounting to open tyranny or oppression. These reports," he continues, "are promptly communicated to the Durbar at Baroda, and have, as a rule, been as promptly attended to, and the grievances brought to light redressed." Referring to some administrative reform introduced by his predecessor's influence, and which, for some time, it required a little watchfulness to maintain, he says, "there will be no resistance to its continuance, for Native States are never prone to alter arrangements they have become used to." The recently appointed Minister he describes as "a man of good character, highly esteemed by the Gaekwar," and under

---

* The admonitions of the Governor-General have of course precluded any future resort to this ancient mode of execution.

† *Ante*, p. 117.

his rule "the State continues to be managed generally to suit our views."

He then refers to the circular from the Under Secretary to the Government of India " on the comparative merits of British and Native rule," intended by Sir John Lawrence to crush Lord Cranborne; and his testimony tends to relieve the Gaekwar's Government from the effect of some strictures in that Correspondence which the Calcutta Editor considers to be too lenient to Native rule.

As in duty bound, and as might naturally be expected, he declares that "the superiority of the British system of rule over that of the Gaekwar, or any other purely Native rule I have known, is, in my opinion clear, and not to be doubted; and yet," he adds, "I believe that the people of India do find something in the courts of Native Princes which compensates for the better administration under our own immediate government." Probably, he suggests, " they find favour from the careers which they open out to Natives of the middle and higher classes."*

In the letter from Calcutta which appeared in the *Times* of the 27th October, 1868, the writer takes the text of the famine now impending over the North West of India, to insult Holkar, Scindia, and the Maharajah of Joudpoor, the largest State of Rajpootana, and repeats his usual sweeping invective against all Native Sovereigns, who, according to him, "oppress fifty millions of Her Majesty's Indian subjects." Speaking of the distress already prevailing in Joudpoor, he says:—

"Such is the oppression of the Maharajah and his myrmidons, that the bands of starving emigrants are plundered of the little money they possess as the only means of subsistence till they reach happier lands."

In the most recent letter from this great public instructor that has reached us at the time I am now writing, published in the *Times* of November 2nd, 1868, he continues his abuse of the Joudpoor Prince, and assures us that "*his*" (the Maharajah's) "*sons live by highway robbery.*"

* *Homeward Mail*, October 26th, 1868.

Some months must elapse before the truth of these foul charges can be tested. In the mean time, after so many specimens, few of my readers will probably be inclined to see more in them than some additional proof of this writer's incurable and unscrupulous intolerance.

The true state of affairs, I believe, is that the Native Princes are making every effort and sacrifice in their power to prevent or mitigate the sufferings of their subjects. It is obviously their interest to do so. We may derive a fair idea of the action likely to be taken in a tolerably well governed Native State when famine is imminent or raging, from the authentic intelligence that has just reached us of the measures adopted by one Prince who has received from time to time his full share of vituperation from the Editor and Correspondent, in both his capacities. The Maharajah Scindia of Gwalior, by a Proclamation dated the 9th September, 1868, has suspended the collection of the public revenue, and issued instructions to all his executive officers well calculated to relieve and employ the people, and to dissuade them from wandering, resorting to mendicancy, or falling into predatory courses.* He has also ordered the disbursement of three lakhs of rupees (£30,000) from his private treasury, for the immediate relief of urgent cases.

The Gwalior Proclamation has been so extensively reproduced, and so warmly praised in all the Indian papers, that even the *Friend of India* could hardly avoid noticing it. Our Correspondent, therefore, gives it at full length in his letter which appears in the *Times* of the 2nd November, and condescends to term it "enlightened and benevolent." In his letter of the preceding week he had included the Maharajah Scindia among the Native Sovereigns who "oppress fifty millions of Her Majesty's subjects." The tone and effect of his letters will be wonderfully changed if he begins to give us authentic intelligence instead of random abuse.

We have seen "our own Correspondent" insulting the late Maharajah of Mysore by calling him a "tyrannical sensualist." That expression, with slight variations of

* *Appendix* C.

intensity, pervades the columns of the *Friend of India* as a sort of synonym for a Native Prince. His wholesale execration of the government of "an idolatrous Hindoo or sensual Mussulman," has already been quoted.* Sometimes they are all heaped together, as in an article in the *Friend of India* of the 23rd of July, 1868, as "Asiatic tyrants and sensualists." Without a plentiful use of these pleasing epithets, and a liberal employment of the term "*effete*,"—" effete Durbars,"† " effete Princelings,"‡ and so forth,—the diatribes against our Allies and feudatories would make but a poor rhetorical show, either in their original humble form, or in the large type of the *Times.*

The application of the customary phrase to the late Rajah of Mysore was peculiarly unfortunate; for Lord William Bentinck, after receiving that Report of the Special Committee of 1833, which, by his own candid acknowledgment, proved the hastiness and harshness of the Rajah's supersession from power, and after his own personal inquiries and observation in Mysore, declared that his Highness's "disposition was *the reverse of tyrannical,*" that he was "in the highest degree intelligent and sensible,". and would "make a good ruler in future."§ The Rajah was in fact universally respected throughout his long reign, by all classes of his subjects, and by every English officer who came in contact with him, for his humane and beneficent character.

It would really appear that the Editor of the *Friend of India* applies these foul names to Native Princes, just as penny-a-liners at home apply a set of stereotyped adjectives to certain functionaries and dignitaries. A reporter to the *Times* cannot mention a Major or a Colonel without prefixing the word "gallant," cannot speak of an Alderman or Magistrate without calling him "worthy;" so the Calcutta Correspondent cannot introduce a Nawab or Rajah without the honourable additions of "tyrannical" or "sensual." In each case it is an

* *Ante*, p. 113.
† *Times*, August 24th, 1868. ‡ *Ante*, p. 112.
§ *The Mysore Reversion*, (2nd Edition) pp. 23 to 26.

essential part of the writer's style. He feels that it is expected of him by the public amidst which he moves. And "our own Correspondent" is completely in tune, when he is acting as Editor of the Calcutta weekly paper. But when transferred to the pages of the *Times*, where conscious power should ever be tempered by a sense of almost national responsibility, his indiscriminate abuse has always appeared to me unsuitable alike to the stage and the audience, utterly out of place in the metropolis of the Empire, strangely out of harmony with the advised sentiments of the great journal itself.

That this writer has got into the way of tacking some vile expletive to the name of every Native Prince he mentions, from sheer force of bad habit, in blind obedience to the insolent bigotry of his class, is most easily proved by calling him in evidence against himself. He repeatedly brands the Rajah of Mysore, without a shadow of cause or excuse, as "a tyrannical sensualist,"—though the slightest inquiry or research would have shown the falsity of both imputations,—but when it suits his purpose, he can draw a very different picture of that Prince, evidently derived from official information. In his letter to the *Times* of the 24th of August, 1868, he wants to prove that the Rajah's large expenditure cannot be accounted for without supposing that enormous sums were wasted in agitating his claims, and those of his adopted son ; and he therefore states with perfect truth that his Highness's "*own tastes were of the simplest kind.*" Tyrannical sensualism can hardly be included among the simplest kind of tastes. That elegant phrase certainly conveys the notion of a somewhat expensive career.

One constant object of the *Friend of India's* insults and menaces is the Maharajah of Cashmere, the same faithful feudatory of whom Lord Dalhousie playfully remarked that he could "crush him at his will ;"* whose troops are now cooperating with General Wilde's Force, and who, as we learn from the most recent intelligence,† has sent 2000 mules to strengthen the British baggage train. The Editor, in the *Times* of the 8th April, 1867, stigmatises

* *Ante*, p. 91. † The *Mofussilite*, August 22nd. 1868.

this Prince as "the *Sultan* of Cashmere, who grinds his people—*our* people, Her Majesty's subjects—to the dust."

In the *Friend of India* of the 13th February, 1868, referring to a long standing restriction by which European travellers are excluded from Cashmere during the winter months, the Editor writes :—

"The Maharajah must be taught that he is a subject although a noble—as much a subject as Scindia or Holkar, over every inch of whose estates an Englishman may travel with a freedom unknown even in England."

This able Editor, a true champion of the English loafer class in India, would make very free with Cashmere, and all Native States ; he wants "a freedom unknown even in England,"—no law, in short, for Englishmen beyond the original jurisdiction of the High Courts.*

The annexation of Cashmere has been frequently advocated by the *Friend of India*, but not, I think, very lately. With some notion, perhaps, of the length to which the Calcutta Foreign Office is prepared to go, his own recent proposals have not gone beyond a military occupation in force. Another journal, however, the *Indian Public Opinion*, published at Lahore, and very much under the influence of the Punjaub Officials, has repeatedly recommended the extreme measure, as in the following extract :—

"The key of India is as much Kabul as Cashmere, and whilst we should render the rulers of the former country subservient to our interests, we ought without any delay to annex the latter. Expediency, the Maharajah's misgovernment, and his flagrant breach of the Treaty, justify, and in the interests of humanity and statesmanship, demand such an annexation.†

That the official inspiration of the *Friend of India* is still widely believed, and excites a certain amount of alarm in Native States up to this day, may be seen in

* There is not much, unfortunately, as it is.

† I have never seen this journal, and quote at second hand from a Reverend gentleman who advocates the immediate appropriation of this Principality,—*The Wrongs of Cashmere*, by Arthur Brinckman, late Missionary to Cashmere, (Bosworth) 1868, p. 42. Some of the reasons for annexation given by the late Missionary are peculiar, *e. g.* "By annexing Cashmere, we should please the French ; they are the chief buyers of the shawls, which are yearly getting dearer and worse under the extortions and oppression of the Rajah." (p. 23.)

the following translated extract from the *Oudh Akhbar*, a newspaper published at Lucknow in the Hindustani language. I borrow it from the *Friend of India* of the 28th of September, 1868, where the article is given at full length, the Editor being doubtless well satisfied with this evidence of his extensive influence, and of the terror of his name in all "the effete Durbars" of India. The subject of the article is the rumoured advance of Russia to the frontiers of Afghanistan, and the intention attributed to our Government of sending troops into Cashmere, and building a strong fort in that Principality. The writer urges that the British Government might defy all the intrigues of Russia, and of all its enemies, if it could revive throughout India the old confidence in its good faith and straightforward intentions. He goes on to say:—

"Cashmere is of course weak, and can be easily won. The *Friend of India* is always against Cashmere; and because in the time of Lord Dalhousie the ruin of Native States used to be published in the Serampore paper, Hindustani Chiefs do not wish to see any account of Cashmere in that paper. To place the Chief of Cashmere in a position of doubt and suspicion at such a time is not necessary. The difficulty is, that the desires of Government appear crooked to the Chiefs of Hindustan; and in the working out of the designs they appear more so. Let those who admire the policy of Lord Dalhousie look at this weak time."

In the letter from the Calcutta Editor and Correspondent, published in the *Times* of the 27th of October, 1868, in which he attacks the Maharajah of Joudpoor, and slanders Holkar, Scindia and several other Princes by name, he observes, with evident regret, that "the doctrine of annexation is dead," but hints that it may yet "be revived."

At this period of our argument it may be asked, why give us so much of the *Friend of India* and its Editor,— why break that gadfly upon a wheel? Partly on account of his access to the *Times*, which contributes very much to his importance in his own circle; partly on account of his reputed connection with the Calcutta Foreign Office, which forms in fact his stock in trade; partly because the journal he edits really does represent very fairly the average tone and course of opinion prevailing among the official class at the central point of Indian administration.

Secretaries and Boards, clerks and Councillors, may consider themselves justified, individually and collectively, for all that I know, in denying that the *Friend of India*, or any other paper, is "the organ of Government," in the strict meaning of that term. It has long had the credit of being so, and it has never been disavowed. That is where the mischief lies. It has enjoyed the enormous advantage of being able to publish in its editorial columns a letter of thanks from a retiring Governor General, "for the support given to his measures,"*—measures of annexation and confiscation which its peculiar sources of intelligence had several times enabled it to forestall, for the delectation of "the Services," to the terror and discomfiture of Native Princes.

It cannot be denied or doubted, that by means of occasional contributions and communications, a good understanding, more or less constant, has been kept up for years, and is still kept up, between this journal and certain public offices at Calcutta, and that the connection has been sometimes promoted and authorised by very exalted persons. Even so late as the 23rd of July, 1868, the *Friend of India* published in its editorial columns some items extracted from the private accounts of the late Maharajah of Mysore, which could only have arrived from the Secret Department of the Foreign Office, by direction, or with the permission, of the Viceroy, Sir John Lawrence himself.†

It is not, therefore, that I fear the speedy revival of a policy of annexation through the burning eloquence of the *Friend of India*. At home it is powerless. The influence of that journal over our countrymen in the East, is nothing to what it was when it stood almost alone and unrivalled for the quality and style of its articles and criticisms. There are many papers now in India, conducted

* From Lord Dalhousie to the Editor of the *Friend of India*, dated March 3rd, 1856, published in the *Friend* of December 31st, 1867,—see *Retrospects and Prospects of Indian Policy*, p. 200.
† *Appendix* D.

with, to say the least, equal ability, which usefully counteract its local egotism, its narrow bigotry, its arrogance and jealousy, half Creole, half professional. In these days the *Friend of India* represents nothing but Chowringhee,—the English quarter of Calcutta,—it reflects only the predominant notions of an official suburb, the average opinions of a Bengal Civilian, slightly qualified by missionary cant. Unfortunately the executive government of all India is carried on in Calcutta; and for the last five years a Bengal Civilian, in many respects nobly distinguished, but quite *down* to the average in his views of Imperial policy, has been at the head of that Government. Hence we have not been getting on. The hard misunderstanding between the governors and the governed, somewhat mitigated by Lord Canning's latest measures, by the tone and manner of his latest public appearances, almost as much as by the terms of his public allocutions and despatches, is now completely reestablished. Since Lord Canning left India, much has been done to alarm and alienate the leaders of the people, nothing has been done to gain the confidence and support of the middle classes, nothing to secure the passive good will of· the population at large. We have been rapidly getting back into the old groove of professional routine; and the same bad feeling against us is spreading all over the country as was revealed when the Rebellion broke out. And if Bengal Civilianism, with the *Friend of India* for its prophet, is allowed to reign supreme at Calcutta much longer, this bad feeling will widen and strengthen, impeding every well intended reform, preventing all real progress, until in a time of general distress or social excitement, it explodes once more, and shakes the foundations of the Empire.

That is the extent of my apprehension. And if it be called vague and indefinite, I can only say that I have no pretension to foretell times or seasons, or the exact course of events. I only know that you cannot expect to grow figs from thistles, or grapes from thorns, however promising the season may be.

Hitherto we have discussed this case on general grounds; we have argued for the rights of the Wallajah family founded on the hereditary Sovereignty of their ancestor, Mahomed Ali, recognised by us and by the Nawab's former Suzerain, the Nizam, guaranteed by the Treaty of Paris, confirmed by our treaties with him, "his heirs and successors," renewed and confirmed by the Treaty of 1801, with the Nawab Azeem-ood-Dowlah, Prince Azeem Jah's father. We have also demonstrated the great loss to the honour of the British Crown, the corruption of our territorial title, the elements of instability, irritation and lawlessness introduced into the political and social system of India, by such a denial of justice as that now under consideration.

Before concluding my task it seems necessary to say a few words on the personal claims and position of Prince Azeem Jah. In the first place it must be observed that this is no doubtful case of an adopted son or distant collateral relative. Prince Azeem Jah is the eldest lineal male descendant of the founder of the dynasty, Anwar-ooddeen Khan. He is the son and brother of reigning Nawabs. When Lord Hastings, in 1813, personally reassured the Nawab Azeem-ood-Dowlah, as to the sacredness of the Treaty of 1801, and the perfect security of himself and his family under its provisions, Prince Azeem Jah was present, and although then quite a child,—he was eleven years old,—has preserved a vivid recollection of what took place. He was himself commended by his father to the protection of the Governor-General, who thus describes the concluding part of an interview with the Nawab at Madras :—

"He asked whether I wished to have his two sons under my eye at Calcutta, as Lord Cornwallis had had the children of Tippoo. I answered that the case was widely different between a vanquished enemy and the representative of a family which had always preserved the most faithful alliance; and added that nothing should induce me ever to give a colour for others to imply a doubt which I myself could not for an instant entertain."*

* *Private Journal of the Marquis of Hastings*, (1858) vol. ii, p. 11. See Appendix B.

K

When the Nawab, by an expressive Oriental obeisance, threw himself and his children under the guardianship of the Governor-General, Lord Hastings observes that he felt the most lively emotion, "from the reflection on the altered state of that family through its adherence to British interests,"—"a family so grievously humiliated by us."

"The Nawab," says Lord Hastings, "having adverted to the Treaty, and professed his anxiety for an assurance that I should cause its provisions to be observed;"—"I answered that a treaty plighted the faith of the nation, so that it must be my duty to maintain its terms according to their true spirit, which ought always to be construed most favourably for the party whose sole dependence was on the honour of the other."*

When we remark the frequent allusions made by the Nawab in these two interviews to his sons and family, and when we call to mind that on his death in 1819, Lord Hastings at once recognised the succession of his son, and declared him to be "a party to the Treaty," there can be no doubt or question as to the meaning and effect of the reassurances addressed by that distinguished soldier and statesman in Prince Azeem Jah's presence to his father, regarding "the true spirit" and "strict observance" of the Treaty of 1801.

By a description of some circumstances and declarations affecting the installation and public life of three successive Nawabs, I have already shown that for the space of fifty-four years no intimation had ever been made to the Carnatic family that they were without hereditary rights, but that on the contrary everything was done to confirm them in the opposite conviction. Prince Azeem Jah himself received, in his public capacity as Regent during the infancy of his nephew, letters from King George IV, and from the Court of Directors, in which the hereditary rights of the family are fully admitted. The following words occur in His Majesty's letter, which is counter-signed by Lord Ellenborough as President of the Board of Control:—

* Appendix B.

"We cannot but admire the beneficent dispensation of Providence, which in taking from his Highness his illustrious father, has given him in your Highness a second father, endowed with equal virtues, *and capable of maintaining in the splendour and dignity which are its inheritance, the illustrious House of the Nabobs of the Carnatic.*"

The language of the letter from the Court of Directors is equally unequivocal on the point of hereditary right.

"The accession of Gholam Mahomed Ghous Bahadoor, the legitimate son of the late Nabob, *to the throne of his ancestors,* we readily confirmed, and we pray God that he may long live to enjoy the honours *and perpetuate the line of the ancient and illustrious family of which he is the descendant and heir.*"

Moreover, during the life-time of his nephew, Prince Azeem Jah had been recognised, both by the Home authorities and by the local Government, in public documents which were officially communicated to him, as the heir presumptive to the Musnud. In a letter dated the 14th of January, 1829, the Court of Directors express their approval of certain acts of the Madras Government, on the ground that Prince Azeem Jah is "*the next heir* in case of the Nabob's demise."* In his proceedings of the 29th September, 1843, the Governor (the Marquis of Tweeddale), in Council, caused the Prince's name to be placed first in the list of persons exempted from judicial process, "in consideration of the position he has lately occupied in communication with the British Government, and that which he still holds in relation to his Highness the Nawab, and *to his succession to the Musnud.*"†

Lord Dalhousie disposed of these recorded acknowledgments of the Nawab's dignity being hereditary, and of Prince Azeem Jah being the next heir, by the following magnanimous argument, a fair specimen of the political casuistry which carried everything before it in the conclaves of Calcutta and Madras :—

"To indicate an expectation, or even an intention, is not to recognise or confer a right. The words, therefore, which have been quoted, conferred no right on Azeem Jah, and conveyed no pledge

* *Carnatic Papers,,* 1860, p. 15.   † *Ibid.*, pp. 8, 9.

or promise to him; and although they indicated a favourable intention of the Government towards him, the Government has since had but too much reason to forego all such intentions in favour of himself and the members of his family."*

Reserving for future treatment the calumnious inuendo conveyed in the latter part of this passage, let us see what the argument itself is worth. It is obvious that Lord Dalhousie completely misconceives the significance of these incidental admissions of hereditary right. Undoubtedly, "to indicate an expectation or an intention"does not "confer" a right, but it certainly does constitute the plainest possible recognition of its existence and validity. Prince Azeem Jah never professed to found his claim on those incidental admissions. He based his right on the hereditary nature of the Nawab's dignity, secured by the Treaties concluded with his ancestors and his father; and he produced these more recent documents simply to prove what was the actual construction put upon those Treaties, only five years before Lord Dalhousie's arrival in India, by the very British authorities who now, under Lord Dalhousie's instructions, denied their binding force.

In describing Prince Azeem Jah's personal position and experiences, I shall make no more than this passing allusion to the disappointment, the mortification, the cruel anxiety, the hope deferred that maketh the heart sick, the ruin or removal of old followers of the family, because, when his right of succession was denied, these results may have been expected, and may have been considered inevitable. I shall speak here solely of those changes and consequences, injurious and painful to the Prince and his family, discreditable to the British Government, which were not foreseen at the time of the late Nawab's decease, and which Lord Dalhousie and Lord Harris may receive full credit for not having intended.

Firstly,—before the death of his nephew, Prince Azeem Jah's character was irreproachable. Whatever errors of judgment he may have committed in his public capacity as Regent during the late Nawab's minority, had been condoned and atoned for, and ought never to have been

* *Carnatic Papers*, 1860, p. 35.

recalled to his prejudice. His moral reputation was unsullied. In the proceedings for effecting and vindicating his deposition and the confiscation of his property, his character has been blasted; he has been covered with insults and ridicule.

Secondly,—at the time of the late Nawab's decease the Prince did not owe a penny. He is now overwhelmed with debt, and with him, his sons, and every one of his relatives who had property or credit to pledge on his behalf.

On the 25th of July, 1861, Mr. Layard, M.P. for Southwark, drew the attention of the Secretary of State for India to the case of Prince Azeem Jah, declaring that "the Prince had been deprived of his revenues and property most unjustly by the East India Company, although his family had rendered great services to the British in India." "The East India Company," he continued, "offered the Prince a large stipend on condition that he would renounce all his claims. The Nawab refused the condition. Would the right honourable gentleman allow that unfortunate Prince to receive the stipend without prejudice to his claims until an opportunity had been afforded for bringing them forward?" In the course of his remarks, the honourable gentleman said, that "the Prince was in difficult circumstances, and had been compelled to raise money at great disadvantage to meet his necessities," and expressed a fear that "Azeem Jah would be compelled to encumber himself with debts which he would never be able to discharge."*

Mr. Layard's anticipations have been fulfilled to the letter. In common charity to Lord Harris we may assume that *his* visions have been falsified. He must remain responsible for a part of the personal abuse, which was a leading feature in the original process; but, with that exception, Lord Harris, we may be sure, never wished to heap injuries on the Wallajah family. He never designed or foresaw the state of humiliation and misery to which the Prince and his family have been reduced in their downfall. Perhaps the full extent and significance of that

* *Hansard*, vol. clxiv, p. 1508.

downfall, from the position of a family of sovereign rank, possessing a large revenue, Palaces, parks, gardens, country houses, and other property, to the position of a family of pensioners without any definite rank, and without any property at all, never struck Lord Harris. He probably imagined that Prince Azeem Jah would take his punishment quietly, give no trouble after a memorial or two, and the whole affair be forgotten in a couple of years. He did not expect that for eight years the Prince would prefer to keep up a shadow of royal state as a visible appeal, on money borrowed in all directions, on security furnished by his relations and adherents, at interest varying from 24 to 60 per cent., rather than seem to compromise his rights by drawing the stipend of £10,000 per annum, allotted to him for life.* He did not anticipate that the Prince's four sons, every one of his relations who had property or credit to pledge, and several of the hereditary officers and retainers, would also be plunged into debt, exposed to bankruptcy, executions, and all the harassing means of constraint that press most heavily on persons of rank, from their determination to support the head of the Wallajah family in maintaining his just rights.

On the 27th of March, 1867, the husband of the Prince's grand-daughter was arrested, and a bailiff placed in possession of his house, on account of a bond which he had signed on behalf of Prince Azeem Jah, who was compelled to raise money on ruinous terms to prevent his young relative being taken to jail. In the same year two European bailiffs gained access to the Prince's own house, and in seeking to arrest one of his Highness's sons, attempted to break into the Zenana apartments. They were stopped by the Prince's armed attendants, beaten severely with muskets, and expelled by a crowd of the Mussulman populace who had flocked into the Palace-yard. This was very nearly being a serious riot; yet it was considered advisable to take no further notice of it. Anyone acquainted with the feelings and customs of

* The Prince himself is exempt from arrest and from every process of our Courts.

Mahomedans of high rank, and with the deep respect and sympathy felt for them by their co-religionists, will understand what a cruel humiliation this intrusion must have been to Prince Azeem Jah, and how the happy accident of the civil power *not* being properly supported, saved the British Government from what, to say the least, would have been a most embarrassing scandal. If the bailiffs had taken the precaution of coming in greater strength, blood would probably have been shed ; the majesty of the Law would in due course have been vindicated, and Lord Harris would have been still more astonished at the unforeseen results of his economical and moral reform.

Lord Harris can never have expected that when, after eight years' resistance, the Prince was reduced in 1863, by the sheer starvation of his servants and smaller creditors, to draw his pension, now augmented to £15,000 a-year, he would only do so under a formal protest, and would still continue the agitation of his claims.

If Lord Harris and Lord Dalhousie could have obtained the least glimpse into the future consequences of their handiwork,—if they could have conceived the trouble and disgust they were entailing upon their respective successors, three or four deep, and upon the Home Government, I think they would have held their hands.

If they could have anticipated six motions in the House of Commons, and four debates and divisions, on this act of state ; that among other strong opinions passed upon it, a leading Conservative politician, the present Lord Chief Baron of England, would stigmatise it as "an act of rapine," and that a hundred and twenty members of Parliament would, on different occasions, ratify that condemnation by their votes, I think they would have hesitated in their course of retrenchment.

Above all, if they could have foreseen how the pecuniary results of that retrenchment would dwindle away in vain efforts to redress and compensate its manifest iniquity,—how, besides large pensions to the late Nawab's widows, the Prince's stipend, originally fixed at £10,000, with no assured provision for his descendants, would first be raised to £15,000, and then to double that amount,

£30,000 per annum, with a permanent endowment for the family; and how a sum of £150,000 having been squandered by the Madras Government in paying what were really our own debts and not the Prince's, the grant not only failed to add to his Highness's comfort and independence, but placed him in a worse position than before, so that a further grant is now required to carry out the intentions of the Secretary of State,—if all this could have been foreseen, I doubt if even Lord Dalhousie and Lord Harris would have cared to despoil the Wallajah family, and outrage the Mahomedans of Southern India, for the sake of a balance of profit so much smaller than that upon which they calculated.

But let us be perfectly just to Lord Harris; let us make the best and strongest case possible for him,—allow him to speak for himself, and interpret him with perfect fairness. If he were now to be examined, he would doubtless declare that in proposing the disinheritance of Prince Azeem Jah he had higher thoughts than mere retrenchment; that although pecuniary results were not to be despised by him and Lord Dalhousie, after three years of deficit, their chief object was moral and political. In his Minute on the subject, Lord Harris states his objections to maintaining the Nawab's dignity under five heads, which I give in his own words, appending to each a very brief comment.

"I will here state my very decided opinion that these rights and privileges should not be continued, if they can be abrogated without a violation of faith.

1st. On the general principle that the semblance of royalty, without any of the power, is a mockery of authority which must be pernicious."

This is a very vague and abstract objection to an establishment existing under a solemn Treaty, from which we have drawn immense advantages.

"2nd. Because *though there is virtually no divided rule or co-ordinate authority in the government of the country (for these points were finally settled by the Treaty of* 1801*)*, yet some appearance of so baneful a system is still kept up by the continuance of a *quasi* royal family and Court."

This objection is a repetition of the first, with an admission that it has no practical weight.

"3rd. Because the legislation of the country being solely in the hands of the Honourable Court, it is not only anomalous, but prejudicial to the community that a separate authority, *not amenable to the laws*, should be permitted to exist."

This third objection is a repetition of the first and second, adding the unimportant, unessential fact of the Nawab's exemption from our judicial processes.

"4th. Because it is impolitic and unwise to allow a pageant to continue, which *though it has hitherto been politically harmless*, may at any time become a nucleus for sedition and agitation."

The fourth objection is a repetition of the preceding three, with a suggestion of political danger. We have already pointed out the utter imbecility of the notion that by making an influential family poor and discontented, you can prevent it from becoming "a nucleus for intrigue," and the Minute writer himself admits that the notion is contradicted by the experience of half a century.

"5th. Because the habits of life and course of proceeding of the Nawabs have been morally most pernicious, tending to bring high station into disrepute, and favouring the accumulation of an idle and dissipated population in the chief city of the Presidency."*

It is with this fifth objection only that we now have to deal. Having disposed of the general question, we are now inquiring how its treatment hitherto by our Government has affected Prince Azeem Jah particularly and personally. In his fifth objection Lord Harris sets the example of that systematic calumny and detraction, by which it has been sought at once to justify spoliation, and to withdraw public sympathy from its victims. It is identical in force and honesty with the rhetorical missiles of "tyrannical sensualist," "worn-out debauchee," and so forth, thrown at random by the *Friend of India* at every Native Prince that passes. Lord Harris says "the habits of life of the Nawabs have been morally most pernicious, tending to bring high station into disrepute." If these imputations were well founded, instead of being monstrously

* *Carnatic Papers*, 1860, p. 9.

exaggerated, their introduction into a plain question of right and title would still be the most obvious impertinence; unless, indeed, among other novel doctrines relating to treaty engagements, we are to be told that "*a personal treaty*" is a treaty the permanence of which depends on *the personal conduct* and moral character of the weaker party,—a treaty, in short, during good behaviour, of which the stronger party is to be the judge, and terminable, apparently, not during the life of an immoral incumbent, but at his death, so that the heir is deprived for his predecessor's profligacy.

Lord Harris impugns the morality of "*the Nawabs.*" Lord Dalhousie, speaking of the late Nawab, says that "*both he and his family* had disreputably abused the dignity of their position, and the large share of public revenue that had been allotted to them."[*] Both statements are slanderous,—a more decorous term would be inadequate to the offence. Whatever may have been the youthful delinquencies of the late Nawab, who died at the age of thirty-one, no public scandal was ever caused by his alleged irregularities. On the other hand, his predecessors, "*the Nawabs,*" accused by Lord Harris, and "*the family,*" accused by Lord Dalhousie, are quite undeserving of this wholesale denunciation. Prince Azeem Jah's elder brother and father, both of them reigning Nawabs, were, according to their lights and the moral standard of their race and religion, most excellent Princes. There have been, and there are now, many members of "the family" of exemplary life, remarkable for their learning, charity and enlightened regard for popular education and other matters of public interest.

A deliberately expressed opinion in Lord Harris's Minute, as to the incurably evil effects of the creeds prevalent in India, and the inevitably bad morals of "a Native Prince, either Hindoo or Mahomedan,"[†] shows to how large an extent that British Governor partook of the ignorant bigotry displayed to perfection by the *Friend of India*,

---

[*] *Minute by the Marquis of Dalhousie*, 28th February, 1856, paragraph 43.
[†] *Carnatic Papers*, 1860, p. 14.

which can see nothing good from Dan to Beersheba, unless it comes of our own race and our own religion, and which, above all, pronounces that every Native Prince must be " a tyrannical sensualist," unless he has received a " Christian education."*

In another part of the same Minute, Lord Harris includes Prince Azeem Jah personally in his attack on the morals of the family in general. He says :—" The rank, consequence and reputation of the Arcot family have sunk by the conduct of its representatives." We have seen by what causes the power and consequence of the family sank under Lord Wellesley's administration,—its royal rank was never impugned,—and but for the utter ignorance of history and his own official records displayed by Lord Harris, we should call his statement as ungenerous as it certainly is inaccurate. He goes on to say :—

"The manner of life and the character of the late Nawab were disreputable; and the conduct of the Prince Azeem Jah, who would succeed him, has already come under the severe animadversion of the Honourable Court."†

Assuming that the current rumours as to the late Nawab's licentiousness were well founded, " the conduct of Prince Azeem Jah" ought not to have been coupled in the same sentence with that of his nephew, as if their " manner of life" had been the same. The Prince's private character and domestic habits have always been decorous and respectable. The "severe animadversion of the Honourable Court," which the Prince brought down on himself in the year 1842, thirteen years before the time when Lord Harris wrote this Minute, did not refer to the Prince's private life, but to his official mismanagement, as Regent, of the Nawab's finances. That mismanagement never cost our Government one penny, and was in fact chiefly caused by the selfish negligence of the British authorities at Madras. Prince Azeem Jah, at the age of twenty-three, quite unqualified and totally inexperienced, was placed in charge of the infant Nawab's affairs, without any check or control of any sort being imposed by our Govern-

* *Ante*, p. 113.
† *Carnatic Papers*, 1860, p. 13.

ment,—at first without any condition expressed in words or writing, afterwards, when a large sum had been advanced to clear off old encumbrances, with the single condition that no new debt should be incurred "without the privity and consent" of the Madras Government. This single condition, to enforce which no means whatever were employed by the Madras Government during the sixteen years of the Regency, the Prince failed to observe. That was the full extent of his error, and grievously was he made to suffer for it. He was led into this error by feelings very natural to a Mussulman of high rank, and especially to one standing in the relation that he did to the principal ladies of the family. He was heavily weighted as Regent with two Dowagers,—the one his own mother, entitled the Nawab Begum, a lady of vast influence and most imperious disposition, the other his brother's widow, who was commonly called the Bhow Begum. These two ladies having contracted expensive habits, and formed large establishments while their respective husbands were on the throne, became deeply embarrassed during the minority; their stipends were consumed by the enormous interest they had to pay for loans, and they were driven to the most humiliating shifts, from which they begged and insisted that the Prince should extricate them. He applied to the Governor of Madras for assistance, but got nothing but good advice. An English officer in charge of the Nawab's affairs might have kept these ladies in order: the Prince was powerless in opposition to his own mother. In reply to one of the Governor's letters he wrote on the 23rd November, 1831:

"I beg to state that I see no possibility of curtailing the monthly allowances of their Highnesses, the Nawab Begum and Bhow Begum, for they can now hardly manage their monthly expenses with their present income, while for their unavoidable and contingent charges they are involved in debts, and which they cannot defray unless they are assisted from the Sircar Treasury."

In the year 1836, when the two Begums' affairs came to a crisis, his Highness took a course which was decidedly wrong, but which the circumstances in which he was placed in some degree explain and excuse. He was "Naib-i-

Mookhtar" (or Absolute Deputy, with full powers) and there can be no doubt that he lawfully possessed the power he exercised. He issued Sircar bonds to the creditors of the two ladies, bearing interest at six per cent., which satisfied the creditors and prevented their ruinous exactions. It was arranged that the bonds should be liquidated by instalments out of the ladies' stipends. The Government was not officially informed of this transaction—a breach of promise which of course cannot be justified, but which admits of extenuation.

The consequence was, that when the Prince came to give an account of his stewardship in 1842, five lakhs of rupees (£50,000) that ought to have been found in hard cash in the Treasury, appeared only in the form of a promissory note payable by the Nawab's grandmother. This was liquidated in a few years by instalments taken from her stipend and that of the Prince Azeem Jah himself, so that his nephew was no loser in the end. The young Nawab, also, entirely repudiated the bonds that had been issued to cover the Dowagers' liabilities, and threw them upon the shoulders of his uncle, the Regent; and these formed "the unsecured debts" of Prince Azeem Jah, of which we shall hear more anon. To make these transactions quite intelligible, it may be usefully explained here that the Nawab, as Sovereign, was exempt from the process of our Courts, and had jurisdiction over certain members of his own family, including Prince Azeem Jah, who were likewise so exempt.

On attaining his majority the late Nawab was greatly incensed against his uncle, their differences being aggravated by a desperate quarrel which broke out between the two Dowagers who had done all the mischief. Eventually, however, the uncle and nephew were reconciled; and it was fully acknowledged by the Nawab, (as indeed by every one who has carefully examined the accounts) that the Prince came out of the office of Regent no richer than when he entered upon it.

It is furthermore worthy of remark that a comparison of the Prince's administration of the Carnatic Sircar with that of his father, brother and nephew, is greatly in his favour. The errors which he committed are fairly attributable to his want of administrative capacity, to the domineering influence of his mother, to his amiable desire to save her and the young Nawab's mother from unaccustomed humiliation, and, above all, to that culpable indifference of our Government to the welfare of their Ward, which left both the care of his estate and the culture of his mind, to the chances of a polygamous household.

Such being the true state of the case as to the only fault of Prince Azeem Jah that had ever exposed him to the animadversion of any British Governor, until he was found guilty in 1857 of unfriendly behaviour in allowing his servants to look hungry, it will, I think, be admitted that he was hardly treated by Lord Harris when that noble lord subjected him to the same condemnation as his nephew, and branded them both as "disreputable." Still more bitter was the phrase employed by the Court of Directors, who, taking their cue from Lord Dalhousie, in their despatch approving and confirming his decision in this case, speak of "the scandalous want of principle evinced in pecuniary matters both by the late Nawab, and by his uncle, Azeem Jah, the nearest collateral relative."* This exaggerated language finds its only explanation in the common tendency of individuals and bodies of men, to cover their acts of injustice, even from themselves, by execrating the injured parties.

Lord Dalhousie, also, besides denouncing "the family" in one Minute as "having disreputably abused the dignity of their position,"† contrives in another, without using any plainer terms, or bringing any specific charge,—which was, indeed, impossible,—to concentrate all the effect of the invective on Prince Azeem Jah's devoted head. In the paragraph already quoted,‡ where he tries to destroy the force of the recognition of Prince Azeem Jah as heir presumptive, Lord Dalhousie gratuitously suggests that there was "a favourable intention" towards the Prince in 1843, in order that he may in some measure account for the altered views of our Government in 1856. He says :—"The

* *Carnatic Papers*, 1860, p. 46. † *Ante*, p. 138.
‡ *Ante*, pp. 131, 132.

Government has since had too much reason to forego all such intentions in favour of himself and the members of his family." This imputation cannot be fitly or adequately characterised as unfair: it is positively untrue. It declares that Prince Azeem Jah "himself" in particular, and "the members of his family," having behaved so well down to 1843 that the British Government had "a favourable intention" towards them, behaved so badly at some period "since," that the Government had "too much reason to forego all such intentions" in their "favour." All this is utterly without foundation or pretext. The conduct of Prince Azeem Jah, of his nephew the late Nawab, and the members of his family, in their relations with our Government, since 1843, had been positively faultless. Lord Dalhousie cannot here be held to refer to the alleged immorality of the late Nawab's private life, for he is expressly speaking of Prince Azeem Jah.

Nor is the case improved if we suppose Lord Dalhousie to have referred to Prince Azeem Jah's "reckless prodigality." That was *before* 1843, not "*since*." The Prince's Regency terminated, and the young Nawab was installed, in 1842; and it was then that Prince Azeem Jah fell under the temporary displeasure both of his nephew and the British Government, in consequence of the unsatisfactory state of his balance-sheet. So that instead of there having been "a favourable intention" towards Prince Azeem Jah, as Lord Dalhousie pretended, in 1843, when our Government registered his name as that of the next in succession to the Musnud, he was then entirely out of favour, and decidedly in disgrace.

Besides these most unjust attacks upon the general reputation of the Wallajah family, and upon the private character of their representative head, another plan,—so invariably adopted in these cases of disinheritance as to seem instinctive to the official mind,—has been assiduously employed, to discredit the cause, and degrade the complainant. This is the plan of boldly asserting the acquiescence of the principal party, who is represented as a passive creature, an utter imbecile, or a worn-out debauchee; while any appeal or agitation that may be raised on his behalf, is attributed to the interested intrigues of "the unprincipled rascals" and "scoundrels,"* who surround the poor dupe and prey upon him. Thus at the very time that Prince Azeem Jah was upholding and prosecuting his claim, amidst a thousand difficulties, to the best of his means and ability, certain Madras officials were busily engaged in casting ridicule and contempt at once upon his cause and his character by the most unqualified declarations that he had abandoned all hope, and had openly avowed his personal indifference.

In the Parliamentary Papers printed in April 1860, which for the first time revealed to him the preposterous prevarications—as they must have appeared in his eyes, —by which he was deprived of his inheritance, Prince Azeem Jah found himself represented to Parliament and the public, as "perfectly understanding and acquiescing in his new position," as having "abandoned the chimerical idea of the restoration of the Nawabship, and accepted his position as the first Native nobleman of Madras."† And yet up to that time he had, as he continued to do until fairly starved out in 1863, steadily refused to touch the stipend allotted to him, and had never ceased, by all the means in his power, to maintain his manifest rights.

Two years later Sir Charles Wood, in his despatch to the Government of Madras of the 8th April, 1862,‡ writes as follows :—

"I learn with regret from these papers, that the Prince has not, as I had been led by Sir Charles Trevelyan to believe, 'accepted his position as the first Native nobleman of Madras,' but is still seeking the restoration in his person of the Nawabship of the Carnatic."

How Sir Charles Trevelyan himself had been misled in the first instance I cannot pretend to divine; but it is remarkable that he seems to have attached some importance to Prince Azeem Jah having "cordially responded" to an invitation to a ball given by the Governor "in celebration of Her Majesty's birthday."

---

* These elegant expressions are culled from a Minute (unpublished as yet) by a Member of Council at Madras.
† *Carnatic Papers*, 1860, p. 50.   ‡ *Appendix* A.

In spite of the "regret," almost equivalent to a reproof, expressed by the Secretary of State, when the Prince's renewed protest contradicted his imaginary submission, another year had scarcely passed when the Agent at Chepauk, through whom an official communication is kept up with the Wallajah family, again wrote to the Madras Government declaring that the Prince had given up all hope of his succession to the musnud being acknowledged, and again urged that his Highness's acceptance of the Governor's hospitality ought to be considered as a sign of acquiescence and resignation. The letter, which has been officially printed but not published, is dated the 7th March, 1863, and the passages in question are as follows:—

"His Highness openly avows" (!) "that he himself is personally indifferent to the result of his pretension to the titular musnud of the Carnatic, and professes that he urges that pretension merely at the instance of his family, and in consideration for their interests. I believe that this is the case,"—(if '*openly avowed*,' what doubt could there be?)—" and that neither the Prince himself nor any of his family have any hope or expectation of the decision recently given in that matter being reversed.

"It cannot be overlooked that the final decision as to the titular musnud was communicated to his Highness nearly a year ago. Had his Highness really thought of seriously contesting that question further, it appears unaccountable that he should have taken no steps in the matter till now, *and that he should have accepted the position assigned him in that decision by attending the Government Ball of the 1st of January of this year.*"

Two motions in favour of Prince Azeem Jah's claim were made in the House of Commons in the year 1863,— that of the Right Hon. H. J. Baillie, on the 26th of February, and that of Sir Fitzroy Kelly, on the 7th of July,—and although the news of the former could only have reached Madras by telegraph, and the latter had not taken place, when the letter just quoted was written, it is clear that its purport is quite erroneous, and that at that particular period of all others the Prince had no reason whatever to despair of obtaining redress.

Nor ought these declarations, originally put forth in secret official communications, but destined, in many in-

L

stances, to be laid before Parliament and the public in Blue Books, to be regarded as insignificant and ineffective. By suggesting hopelessness, and imputing indifference, by misinterpreting the commonest act of civility, or expression of allegiance, into acquiescence in the inferior position forced upon the claimant, these declarations were well calculated to distract attention from the strength of the claim, to compromise the Prince's dignity, especially among his own countrymen, and to destroy all sympathy for his personal wrongs.

In an earlier page of this treatise I have said that our Government, in its treatment of Prince Azeem Jah, has revived, renewed and confirmed the prevailing tradition as to our treatment of the Wallajah family down to the Treaty of 1801, and has played over again before the people of Southern India the old scenes of dethronement, defamation and pillage.* The dethronement has been made sufficiently clear. We have just examined the process which Mussulman fanatics call defamation, and may now take a glance at the transactions which the benighted Hindoos call pillage.

It will be remembered that Sir Charles Wood, in the debate of 26th of February, 1863, denied that there had been any dethronement or annexation at all. "In 1801," he said, "the Nawab was reduced to the rank of a pensioner at Madras,"† If then the Nawab of the Carnatic was merely a pensioner,—a private person of high rank, —how came it that at the death of the late Nawab, our Government practically ruled that he could possess no private property, and swept every convertible asset into its own Treasury ? On what principle did the British Government, after refusing to recognise Prince Azeem Jah as successor to the Sovereignty of his ancestors, also refuse to recognise him as heir to the family property, real and personal ?

* *Ante*, p. 47.   †*Ante*, p. 1.

This looks very much as if we alternately depressed the Nawab to "a mere pensioner"—"a dependent of rank," as Lord Harris termed him,*—when we wished to renounce our Treaties, and exalted him to "an independent Sovereign," when we wanted to lay hands on his property, and claim it for the State.

It has been proved in these pages beyond all possibility of further dispute, that the Nawab was in fact a Sovereign Prince, and not "a mere pensioner."† Our opponents may, perhaps, admit so much, shift their ground entirely, and assert that, by the very fact of his Sovereignty, the Nawab was incapable of holding private property, and that everything he possessed was public property, and belonged to the State. Such an argument will not bear a moment's examination. The Nawab, although entitled to a certain income under Treaty, had nothing to do with the receipt, administration, or expenditure of public revenue. His income was strictly of the nature of a Privy Purse, entirely at his own disposal, for the benefit of himself and his family.

No reasons of even tolerable plausibility were ever advanced to show that any of the lands or houses, cash or valuables, in the Nawab's possession were public property. From some scruple of pride, or apprehension of compromising his claim to the Sovereignty, Prince Azeem Jah, after protesting formally against our appropriation of the estate, refrained from submitting the case to a judicial decision. Thus the question has never been argued. Everything was assumed to lie at the mercy of our Government, and the strangest confusion is manifest in the official statements on the subject. For instance, the Madras Government propose, and the Court of Directors approve it, that "the personal property of the Nabob be turned into money, and applied to" the payment of his debts, but that "the property clearly belonging to the Sircar, such as the Chepauk Palace, &c., should revert to Government."‡ The Court of Directors feel that there is something wrong, or

* *Carnatic Papers*, 1860, p. 13.
† *Ante*, pp. 3 to 7, and 25 to 31.
‡ *Carnatic Papers*, 1860, pp. 6, 15, 18, 46.

at least doubtful here, for "Sir Henry Montgomery," they remark, "says that it," the Palace, "was mortgaged, which might imply that it was considered to be private property."*

If any part of the Nawab's real estate could be considered more distinctly private property than another, it was Chepauk Palace. Built more than a hundred years ago by the Nawab Wallajah, on ground which he purchased at Madras, this Palace was not even situated within the limits of his Government. No Nawab of the Carnatic, whatever may have been his claim of Suzerainty and tribute, ever pretended to exercise jurisdiction within the Town of Madras. The land on which the British settlement stood had been purchased from the Hindoo Rajah of Chandraghiri in the year 1639, many years before the Mogul Emperor established his authority in that Province. The Nawab Wallajah and his son Omdut-ool-Oomra, the last two of the family who exercised the active functions of Sovereignty, preferred to reside usually at Madras in their Palace of Chepauk, but they had to travel a mile or two before they arrived at the first village where their direct commands were obeyed. No Palace, therefore, could be more clearly a private residence. Nor could it, I presume, have become public or State property while each mediatised successor of the Nawab Omdut-ool-Oomra continued to reside there, secured by the provisions of the Treaty of 1801, in "the rank, property and possessions of his ancestors."

It does not seem to be a principle accepted in Europe that Sovereigns can have no private property. The daily papers of July 13th, 1868, all contained this scrap of news from Vienna,

"The Italian Government has paid to the Austrian ambassador at Florence the sums being part of the private fortune of the Archdukes, formerly Sovereigns in Italy. The interest alone amounts to two million lire."

Neither the Italian Government nor the Italian people had much reason to deal tenderly with the Archdukes.

* *Carnatic Papers*, 1860, p. 46.

Neither the British Government, nor the people of the Carnatic, have ever had any quarrel with the Wallajah family.

It may be said, however, that a full justification for appropriating the late Nawab's property can be easily made out, for the British Government undertook the payment of his debts. Sir Charles Wood, in his despatch of 8th April, 1862, said :—" By the aid of a special legislative enactment, the debts of the Nawab have been paid in full."* He ought to have said that by the aid of an act of pillage the debts of the Nawab had been paid, and that a special legislative enactment had been passed to give that act of pillage the force and forms of law.

The Government, it is said, has paid the Nawab's debts. The portion of the Nawab's debts paid by our Government amounted to £330,000, little more than two years' income. Those debts were contracted on the credit of the Nawab's revenue, not on the credit of his real or personal estate ; and when our Government was pleased to sequestrate that revenue, granting pensions for life to the widows and other relatives, they were clearly bound to answer for the debts. But they were not satisfied with the revenue ; they confiscated everything that could be turned into cash. All the lands, gardens, buildings and personal property belonging to the family, every relic and heirloom, down to the Musnud of state and other insignia of the Nawab's dignity, were either appropriated to the purposes of our Government, or sold for their benefit, for the most part at prices far below the real value. In this way about £180,000, more than half the amount paid, was raised. The principal Palace of Chepauk, where Prince Azeem Jah was born, and the last three Nawabs, his father, brother and nephew, died,—is turned into a range of Public Offices, while the Prince is compelled to pay rent for one of the minor residences, granted for his use by the late Nawab, and which he has occupied for the last forty years.

And it would seem as if there were still some receipts

---

* *Appendix* A.

expected, beyond the sum of £180,000, which our Government is understood to have realised. We read in the *Homeward Mail* of the 5th October, 1868, that at the meeting of the Viceroy's Legislative Council on July 20th, Mr. Maine introduced a Bill to re-appoint a Receiver of the property of the late Nawab of the Carnatic. "Considerable assets belonging to the late Nawab's estate have been recently secured both in Madras and the Nizam's territories, and it thus becomes necessary to revive the office of Receiver."

In the face of these facts our Government deserves little credit for having paid the Nawab's debts. But our Government deserves still less credit in the face of the fact that it repudiated a great part of the Nawab's debts, and threw the burden upon Prince Azeem Jah. It deserves still less credit in the face of the fact that the debts which it repudiated, and threw upon Prince Azeem Jah, were charged to our Government by a judicial decision of the Supreme Court of Madras; and that a second "special legislative enactment" was passed, expressly to nullify the effect of that judicial decision, and to shift the burden of those debts from its own shoulders to those of the Prince who had already been stripped of his inheritance,—both of the income payable under Treaty, and of the family estate. When this second special legislative enactment, specially designed to defeat the decision of the Court, was passed, by the aid of the electric telegraph, all the standing orders being suspended, some of the claimants under the original Act applied for postponement, in order to enable them to petition the Home Government for the disallowance of the new Act, and in giving judgment, on the 8th August, 1859, the Chief Justice, Sir Henry Davison and his colleague, Sir Adam Bittleston, spoke in the strongest condemnatory language of the object for which the Act was passed and the manner of passing it. The Chief Justice observed:—"Called upon as I am under the peculiar circumstances of this case, I am bound to declare my opinion that the legislation complained of is of the grossest *ex post facto* character, and that it violates the first principles of legislation and of justice."

Sir Adam Bittleston remarked :—

"The claimants under Act 30 of 1858, had and have a right to say that it means that which we held it to mean, and that their claims were filed under that understanding of the Act. True it is that the Legislative Council have not assumed to set aside the decision of this Court in the particular case in which it was pronounced, but they have made the very nearest approach to so doing, by hurriedly interposing an enactment to nullify that decision as to all the subsequent cases standing on the list for hearing, which would have been governed by it. This is a grave matter on public grounds. It is obviously fatal to any confidence in the administration of justice in any of the Courts of this country, if as soon as a decision adverse to the wishes or interests of Government is pronounced, the legislative power may be invoked by the executive authority (the two being very closely allied and linked together) to interpose and nullify such decision."

These liabilities, transferred in this extraordinary manner—so edifying for the benighted Hindoos,—from the confiscating Government to the disinherited Prince, consisted of the Sircar bonds, mentioned in the last Section,* issued by the Regent during the minority of the late Nawab, in satisfaction of claims against the two Dowager Begums, the Nawab's mother and grandmother. Under the special legislative enactments of our Government—of which Sir Charles Wood wrote in his despatch as if they were acts of self-sacrificing generosity,—these liabilities became "the unsecured debts" of Prince Azeem Jah.

What a lesson, what an example for the Indian people whom we have undertaken to raise into a higher sphere of politics and morals! How well calculated our procedure in this Carnatic affair has been to make them a law-abiding people, to teach them reverence for the three branches of our civilised government,—the Executive power, the administration of justice, and the Legislature!

In the course of years, by dint of discussion in Parliament and the press, the mass of misrepresentation and error by which Prince Azeem Jah's rights had been obscured, began to be cleared away; and the unforeseen state of distress and humiliation to which he and his family had been reduced, became more manifest and more scandalous. The authorities at Madras, as well as the Home

* *Ante*, p. 141.

Government, were gradually roused to a conviction that something must be done to set this irrepressible grievance at rest. Certain "officious" negotiations, set on foot with the approval of Sir Charles Wood, (now Lord Halifax) were brought to something like maturity while the present Marquis of Salisbury was in office. Under instructions from the Secretary of State, the Governor of Madras, Lord Napier, addressed Prince Azeem Jah on January 15th, 1867, proposing to make a revised arrangement for the permanent benefit of his Highness and his family, on the understanding that the Prince, on his part, was "disposed to abandon his claim as the heir and successor of the late Nawab."

The more important and substantial of the concessions promised to the Prince, were that the hereditary title of "Prince of Arcot" should be conferred upon him by letters patent from Her Majesty the Queen; that his stipend should be raised from £15,000 to £30,000 per annum for his life,—one half of the latter sum being settled in perpetuity on his linear male descendants in shares, according to their age and position; and that an immediate sum of £150,000 should be granted for the payment of his debts.

It is with this last promised boon that we are now more immediately concerned. It may appear incredible, but is not the less true, that the Government of Madras, having refused to entrust to Prince Azeem Jah the disbursement of the sum of £150,000 assigned for the payment of his debts, and even to consult him as to its disposal, appointed a well paid English Commissioner to administer this fund— from which he drew his own salary—that the greater part of the money—four fifths at least—was expended in paying of the so-called "unsecured debts," which "a special legislative enactment" had imposed upon the Prince, after a British court of justice had declared them payable by our Government.

The object of the Secretary of State in offering this grant, the object of the Prince in accepting the proposal, was that of affording and obtaining relief from the cruel and humiliating pressure upon those nearest and dearest and most faithfully attached to him, arising from the debt contracted since his disinheritance. This object has been completely defeated by the mismanagement of the Madras authorities. The "unsecured debts," the payment of which properly devolved on our Government, and which their Commissioner paid off with the Prince's money, had never produced, and never could have produced the slightest pressure on his Highness or any member of his family. The holders of those securities, mostly purchased at a very low rate, had about as much expectation of being paid a year ago, as the holders of Confederate cotton bonds have now.

Our Government has completely failed to fulfil the promises held out to Prince Azeem Jah. Certainly the sum of £150,000 has never been "granted" to his Highness in any proper acceptation of the word. The money was retained by the local Government, and expended, not only without any reference to the Prince's wishes, but in direct opposition to his advice and warning, in a manner against which he protested as wholly without benefit to himself or his family. The money has been almost entirely thrown away upon the holders of certain old bonds of the Carnatic Sircar, which went indeed by the name of the Prince's "unsecured" debts, but which never gave him any trouble; which could have been settled by a trifling composition, and ought to have been settled by our Government, in accordance with the decision of their own Court of Justice, as the executors and sequestrators of the Nawab's estate and revenue. The payment of these "unsecured" debts was a relief to no one but our Government, and an act of liberality to no one but the delighted speculators, who suddenly found their worthless bonds converted into valuable securities.

But though totally inoperative as a relief to the Prince, the payment of these bonds naturally roused the expectations of the "secured" creditors to the highest pitch. The pressure of their demands has been redoubled by the misappropriation of the funds intended for the Prince's deliverance. The addition recently made to his Highness's income now goes in the partial discharge of interest to stave off the arrest of his relatives or the legal proceedings with which they are threatened. This purgatorial state, under present arrangements, will continue during his lifetime, but on his death the income will be reduced one half, while the hold of the creditors on the family will not cease. His sons are being involved along with him, and will be plunged more deeply into debt, in proportion to their more limited income, than he is at this present moment. In short, according to the present aspect of affairs, the family is ruined for generations by the measures intended by Government for its benefit.*

The Home Government having at last been brought, by the Prince's remonstrances, to a sense of the utter defeat of their plan for his extrication, now, it is said, propose to advance a further sum of £120,000 for the satisfaction of the " secured" creditors,—whose claims have absorbed almost all the Prince's receipts for the last two years in interest,—and to stop one half of his Highness's income, until the amount thus advanced has been recovered. As Prince Azeem Jah is now sixty-six years of age, he would have little prospect, under this arrangement, of enjoying, for even one year, the increased stipend promised to him.

---

* It is this part of the case, and this part only, that has attracted the attention of the *Pall Mall Gazette*, (August 28th, 1868) and of the *Times* (October 10th, 1868) though they both seem to be unacquainted with the true nature of the " unsecured debts," which so much enhances the errors of our executive officers in India. Extracts from these articles will be found in Appendix E.

Both with regard to the payment of his debts, and his augmented income, our Government has failed so completely to execute the terms offered to Prince Azeem Jah, that he might well reject the tacit understanding that he was to abandon the open assertion of his ancestral claims. But whatever may be the force of that tacit understanding during the Prince's life, it can neither destroy the rights, nor silence the claims of his sons, who will begin to feel, on their father's death, when one half of his income is divided between them, the aggravated pressure of the debts, created, as they will say, by our injustice, and perpetuated by our maladministration. One of the most eminent Judges now on the Bench, has declared that "the Treaty of 1801 is an enduring contract, binding on both sides, *so long as there exists any member of the family of the Nawab Azeem-ood-Dowlah, capable of succeeding to the rank.*"*

Prince Azeem Jah has four legitimate sons, all lineal male descendants of the Nawab Azeem-ood-Dowlah, with whom the Treaty of 1801 was concluded, and of the Nawab Wallajah, who was recognised as legitimate Sovereign of the Carnatic by the Treaty of Paris, between the Kings of France and Great Britain in 1763, and by his former Suzerain the Nizam in the Treaty of 1768, and with whom, "*his heirs and successors*," our Treaties of 1787 and 1792, "*renewed and confirmed*" by the Treaty of 1801,

* The opinion of Mr. Lush, Q.C., (now Mr. Justice Lush) refers to much longer and more elaborate opinions by Sir Travers Twiss, now the Queen's Advocate, and the Hon. J. B. Norton, Advocate-General and Member of the Legislative Council at Madras. "I entirely concur in the opinions expressed by Dr. Twiss and Mr. Norton, that the Treaty is an enduring contract, binding on both sides, so long as there exists any member of the family of the Nabob Azeem-ul-Dowlah capable of succeeding to the rank. And I come to this conclusion upon consideration of the terms of the Treaty itself, read with reference to the circumstances under which it was made, and without regard to the Letter, Proclamation and Despatch which followed it. These documents, however, might be called in aid, were the language of the Treaty ambiguous, as a contemporaneous exposition of its meaning. But whether read with or without them, it does not appear to me to admit of any other construction than that contended for by His Highness Azeem Jah."

Temple, December 1st, 1864,   (Signed)   ROBERT LUSH.

were concluded.* If Prince Azeem Jah had happened to die before his nephew, the late Nawab, his eldest son† would have stood all this time exactly in his father's position,—unless we attach any importance to the point once made by Lord Dalhousie in an analogous case, that Azeem Jah was "born in the purple."‡ With this Byzantine difference, the son would have taken precisely the same place as the father; his claim to the succession would have been equally strong. The son's place cannot have been altered, or his contingent claim weakened, by the mere fact that his father out-lived the late Nawab. On the death of Prince Azeem Jah, his eldest surviving son, then the head of the Wallajah family, will stand in the same relation as his father now does, to our Government and to the people of the country, and will inherit the new title, under Royal patent, of Prince of Arcot. On what principle is he only to be allowed—as at present provided, —one quarter of the stipend considered sufficient for his father? Is that income likely to meet his requirements, to render him or his adherents contented, or to make his moderating influence on the side of law and order fully effective?

Sir Charles Wood, now Lord Halifax, expressed the following opinion in the debate of the 26th of February, 1863, on Prince Azeem Jah's claims.

"He must distinctly say that the existence of these pensioned Princes, without power and authority, fancying that they had rights which some day or other they would enjoy, was the most inconvenient state of things, both for the Government and the Princes themselves, that could possibly be conceived."§

Sir Charles Wood has described, in the sentence just quoted, the actual state to which the Wallajah family has been reduced, not their state before the confiscation,—the result of Lord Harris's handiwork, not of Lord Welles-

* *Ante*, pp. 10 and 11.
† Zaheer-ood-Dowlah Mahomed Badee-Oollah Khan.
‡ The eldest son of the King of Delhi having died during his father's life-time, Lord Dalhousie cried down the claim of the next heir, the king's grandson, by observing that he was not "born in the purple!" (*Minute by the Marquis of Dalhousie*, 1856, para. 41, p. 11.)
§ *Hansard*, vol. clxix, p. 816.

ley's. Before the death of the late Nawab, and the disinheritance of the next in succession, there was not, and could not be, any room for "*fancying*" that they had any inconvenient "rights." Their rights were carefully defined and circumscribed by the Treaty of 1801, which, on the other hand, was our sole and sufficient title-deed for the exclusive government of the Carnatic. But a very wide range for "fancy" is opened by our arbitrary violation of that Treaty.

And yet I don't know. What room is there left for "fancy" to these unfortunate Princes? If the defects of our rule have placed their rights in abeyance, the splendour of our liberties has ensured their open discussion, and has displayed them to the world. What room can there be left for "fancy" or doubt in the minds of these Princes, or of those who take an interest in their fate, when they observe that a hundred and twenty Members of Parliament, including several eminent statesmen, have pronounced in their favour?* Can the belief in their hereditary rights be called a "fancy," when it is confirmed by the opinions of three of our own Judges and the Advocate-General of Madras?† If they are inclined to use bitter language with regard to the disinheritance of the late Nawab's lawful successor, can their "fancy" supply a stronger term than that publicly used in the Great Council of the Empire by the present Lord Chief Baron of England, who called it "an act of rapine."

This is unquestionably a very "inconvenient state of things," and it bids fair to be permanent; but it is a direct consequence of the confiscation, and never could have arisen as long as the Treaty of 1801 remained inviolate.

So long as the provisions of the Treaty of 1801 were maintained in force,—until the decease of the late Nawab,—the only incident in the "state of things" that was really found "inconvenient," was the exemption of the reigning Prince and some of his nearest relatives from the jurisdiction of our Courts. This undoubtedly removed the only efficient check on extravagance and mismanage-

* *Ante*, p. 96.   † *Ante*, pp. 96 and 155.

ment, and led to unseemly altercations, which our Government was powerless to reconcile. But our Government had *made itself* powerless. This exemption is not among the provisions of the Treaty of 1801. It rested upon nothing but custom, and was secured by nothing but our own legislation. It is strange that Lord Harris should write of this difficulty as if it had been irremediable, when we learn from the Minute of one of his colleagues in the Madras Government, that a change in the law was contemplated about the time of the late Nawab's death. "So great," says Sir Henry Montgomery, "have been found the embarrassments and injustices thence arising, that within the last few months the Government has been forced into the consideration of some alteration of the law by which the late Nawab was protected from civil process."*

Every practical or imaginable inconvenience in the Nawab's position, every defect in our title, might have been cured,—and may yet be cured,—by a convention with Prince Azeem Jah, by a decisive proclamation, and by appropriate legislation. This could not be done so effectually, or so gracefully, after his death. Many valuable opportunities have passed away: the last may slip by us, if more time is lost.

What cruelty, what wickedness, what political insanity, to foster and propagate a breed of pretenders such as these would be,—justified by Treaties, encouraged by British Statesmen and Judges, the best possible standing provocative for either a popular cry, or a diplomatic cry against us, as occasion might offer. From a Prince to a pretender, from a pretender to a conspirator, from a conspirator to a convict,—the gradations are few. The heir of the Rajah of Sattara, whose administration was declared by the Court of Directors to be "a model to all Native rulers,"† is, or was lately, a state prisoner in Butcher's Island, near Bombay, suspected of a treasonable conspiracy in 1857. The widowed Ranee of Jhansi,—"highly respected and esteemed," "a lady of very high character,"‡—was killed

---

* *Carnatic Papers*, 1860, p. 15.
† *Sattara Papers*, 1843, p. 1268.
‡ *Jhansi Papers*, 1855, pp. 7 and 28.

in battle before the city of Gwalior on the 16th of June, 1858. Her father was hanged. I have never heard what became of her adopted son. Are some of the Wallajah family to embellish the future history of India with incidents like these? Let them look to themselves, it may be said; we are strong enough to deal with them, if they turn against us. We should, doubtless, be strong enough to hang them in such a case, by due form of law,—or by aid of one of those special legislative enactments that were found so efficacious in 1857. But is it not always more satisfactory to be able to do that sort of thing without compunction and with a clear conscience?

The fact is that our modern humanitarian scruples, and our hankering after legality, prevent us from doing this kind of work thoroughly. The only plan for insuring that the Wallajah family should not become "inimical," or a "nucleus for sedition," after their destitution, would have been to put them all to death, or to send them off to perpetual imprisonment. If we are to degrade and despoil great families as the Great Mogul used to do, it must be done in the same style and by the same means as the Great Mogul employed. Oriental violence and British law do not amalgamate pleasantly.

And again, when an error of judgment in the action of our Government, whereby some innocent person has suffered loss or wrong, becomes manifest, our free institutions forbid us to brave it out, and crush all complaint and opposition, as a despot would do. If the injured party were born or were residing in the British Islands, or within the ordinary range of Western opinion, restitution or reinstatement would follow, as a matter of course, on full conviction that wrong had been done. In our relations with Oriental races and personages, with whom we have little social intercourse, and whose affairs in quiet times excite little sympathy or interest in Europe, we have hardly as yet attained to that high standard of justice and morality.

Thus may be explained in a great measure the singular inconsistency and conflict of principles, that pervades the whole history of this case, and characterises especially the more recent efforts at its final settlement. The successive steps we have made towards a compromise, have weakened local authority, without restoring the moral influence of the Crown. The Government of Madras loses credit both by the first and the last operations; the Imperial Government gains by neither. The concessions that have been made are sufficient to quell any doubt in the minds of the Wallajah family as to the fulness of their rights, and as to our perfect knowledge of them, but not sufficient to afford satisfaction or compensation. We have made a sufficient confession to convince all the world of our guilt, but we do not merit and cannot obtain absolution.

It is of no use trying any more to tinker and cobble the shattered fabric of Lord Harris's workmanship. The foundations are rotten; the ground it stands upon is false. But it is not yet too late to reconstruct the old edifice on a solid basis,—on terms acceptable to all parties, honourable and serviceable to the Imperial Government. Some day it will be too late. The ruins may fall, and should they fall at an unlucky time, or in a wrong direction, they will form a stumbling-block and a rock of offence for the ignorant people, a monument of reproach for ever against their enlightened rulers.

POSTSCRIPT.

Since the preceding pages were in type, a copy of the Report of the Central India Agency for the year 1866-7 (published by authority, Calcutta, 1868), just received, has cleared up in a manner most satisfactory to me, certain points where my information was deficient.

At page 117 of this volume I have charged our Calcutta Correspondent and Editor of the *Friend of India*, with "gross exaggeration," for having said in his letter of the 10th of March, 1866, that "Lord Stanley's persistence in causing the restoration of Dhar *has reduced that State to a miserable condition;*" and from such occasional intelligence as has reached me, I ventured to say—"Dhar is going on very well."

Colonel Meade, the Governor General's Agent in Central India, reporting on the Principality of Dhar for the year 1866-7 (paragraph 111, page 19), writes as follows :—

"The general administration of this State has been satisfactory, and the Chief, Anund Rao Powar, takes much interest in, and exercises a general supervision over, its affairs."

There is nothing here, or in any part of the Report, to suggest a "miserable condition."

With reference to the Editor and Correspondent's calumnies against the Prince and State of Indore, noticed by me at page 118, the only additional remark that need be made here, is that in the Report on Central India for 1866-7, nothing but good is said of Maharajah Holkar and his Government.

The Report fully corroborates my surmises as to the painful effect produced on the mind of Maharajah Scindia by the impolitic interference with the distribution of his troops upon which I have commented at page 104 to 111. The measures for the reduction and dispersion of these troops are said to have been taken "in February last,"

(1867), and "a full and detailed Report of the circumstances was furnished" in a despatch dated 15th March, 1867. The Agent, whether he approves or not of Sir John Lawrence's policy in this matter, cannot of course venture to express any doubt or disagreement. He says (para. 62, p. 13), "it would be hardly possible to overstate the soreness caused by the check that has thus been given to the indulgence of his passion for military organisation and parades, and of his desire to keep his whole Force with this object at the capital under his personal control and command."

He continues thus (para. 63):—

"I will only add that this result, however to be lamented, was altogether inevitable; and that the necessity for the adoption of the measures under advertence being deemed imperative under the circumstances, no consideration that I am aware of could have broken, or even mitigated, the effects of the blow to His Highness. Certainly no effort was spared by either the Political Agent or myself with this object."

One would like to hear what were alleged as "the circumstances" that rendered these offensive measures "imperative," and whether it was by the Agent in Central India, or by Sir John Lawrence and Sir Henry Durand at Calcutta, that they were "deemed imperative."

It cannot be considered wonderful after this, that the Agent (para. 65 to 68, pp. 13, 14), while "cordially admitting" Maharajah Scindia's "friendly personal bearing," declaring his Highness to be "accessible and courteous, and prepared to discuss most subjects in a pleasant way, and to listen with attention to the arguments addressed to him," and giving his testimony to "the Maharajah's respect for the authority of the British Government," should still find that the Prince is now and then "suspicious and distrustful," and sometimes "considers the intervention of the British Government, or its officers, unwarrantable." How could it be otherwise while Imperial supremacy was exerted for his personal discomfiture in a manner so offensive and vexatious?

APPENDIX.

(A.)

(Page 81.)

Despatch from the Right Honourable Sir Charles Wood, Bart., Secretary of State for India, to his Excellency the Honourable the Governor in Council, Fort Saint George, Madras, dated London, April 8th, 1862, *No.* 6.

1. I have taken into consideration in Council, the contents of the Memorial of Prince Azeem Jah of the Carnatic family, enclosed in the letter of your Excellency's Government, No. 24 of 1861,* and of its other enclosures relating to his case.

2. I learn with regret from these papers, that the Prince has not, as I had been led by Sir Charles Trevelyan to believe, " accepted his position as the first Native Nobleman of Madras," but is still seeking the restoration in his person of the Nawabship of the Carnatic. In the Memorial now before me, he prays that " he may be restored to, and confirmed in all the rights, titles, dignities, revenues, and property belonging to him as the heir, representative, and successor of the late Nawab of the Carnatic, or that such redress may be adjudged to your Memorialist as shall be doing justice between the Government of India and your Memorialist."

3. Six years have elapsed since the final decision of this case by the Government of India and the Home Authorities. The determination then come to, after full consideration of all the facts and circumstances urged by the Memorialist in his present communication, was that the Treaty of 1801, made with Azeem-ul-Dowlah, having been purely personal to that Prince, and not having been renewed, had no existence subsequently to the death of Azeem-ul-Dowlah in 1819, that the position assigned by the Government in 1819 to his son Azum Jah, and again in 1825 to his grandson Mahomed Ghous Khan, by pure favour of the Government, was personal to those individuals respectively, and was expressly so considered at the time, and that on the death of His Highness Mahomed Ghous Khan, "the title and dignity of Nawab, and all the advantages annexed to it by the Treaty of 1801 were at an end."

4. The decision of the Government, and the grounds upon which that decision was based were communicated to Prince

---

* Dated October 11th.

Azeem Jah* and the other parties interested, by the Madras Government; and the instructions sent to that Government for the payment of the debts due by the late Nawab, and the assignment of allowances on a liberal scale to all dependents and persons entitled to provision from the estate, appear to have been executed in the spirit intended by the Home Government. By the aid of a special legislative enactment, the debts of the Nawab, to the amount of Rupees 33,00,000, (£330,000) have been paid in full, the allowances of the ladies of His Highness's family and old dependents have been continued, and the stipend of the Memorialist has been raised from Rupees 48,000 (£4,800) the sum enjoyed by him in the late Nawab's lifetime, to Rupees 150,000 (£15,000) per annum.

5. A very full, patient, and searching revision of all the papers of this case, and of the arguments adduced by the Memorialist, has convinced me that there are no grounds to justify me in disturbing the decision arrived at six years ago, and advising Her Majesty to re-establish the titular Nawabship of the Carnatic.

6. It is my desire that this final decision on the claims of Prince Azeem Jah may be communicated to him, with all due consideration to his high rank and position. (Signed) C. WOOD.

(B.)

EXTRACT FROM THE PRIVATE JOURNAL OF THE MARQUIS OF HASTINGS IN 1813.

(Page 129.)

"The conversation began by compliments—hopes that I and my family had not suffered by the length of the voyage, and inquiries relative to the King and the Prince Regent. He" (the Nawab) "adverted to the Treaty and professed his anxiety for an assurance that I should cause its provisions to be observed. I had been told that he had been under great alarm, lest I should still further degrade his already abject condition; an apprehension probably entertained from his knowledge that (when the vacancy of the Musnud was impending) application had been made to me in favour of the unfortunate young man, set aside by our Government to make way for this individual. I answered that a Treaty plighted the public faith of the nation, so that it must be my duty to maintain its terms according to their true spirit, which ought always to be construed most favourably for the party whose sole

---

* This was a complete mistake on the part of the Secretary of State; no such communication had been made, or ever has been made to Prince Azeem Jah.—E. B.

dependence was on the honour of the other. He did not attempt to conceal his gratification at this answer. After some desultory conversation he said I had too much business to make it proper for him to trespass longer on me. I then called for otto of roses and rose-water with which I perfumed his handkerchief, gave him *pawn*, and threw round his neck a chaplet of rose-coloured odoriferous flowers. The ceremony I had been instructed to perform without rising from my seat; a point to which the Government here attaches much importance. I went through the same ceremony to the eldest son. Then three other Princes were made to rise, and come up to me for the same compliment, the Nawab being particular in calling each of them to make his obeisance in receiving it.

"The chaplets provided for them were, according to rule, of only white flowers. We descended the stair in the original form. After I had embraced the Nawab at the carriage door, he took hold of both my hands, and stooping very low, placed his head between them, desiring the Persian Secretary to explain, that by that act he threw himself and family under my protection. This was a gesture not indifferent for the Native crowd who witnessed it; yet I know not if it did not excite in me much more lively sensations, from the reflection on the altered state of that family through its adherence to British interests.

"Subsequently the Nawab told the Persian Secretary that he had never been so happy in his life as my expressions respecting the Treaty had made him. He expatiated, with effusions of gratitude, on my tone of politeness, which appeared to me no more than the simple due of humanity towards a family so grievously humiliated by us."

The incidents that took place on the occasion of returning the Nawab's visit, Lord Hastings describes as follows:—

"He then led me to the sofa, placing me on the left (the place of honour with them), and seating himself in the middle, with his eldest son on the right. My suite were placed on chairs in a semicircle to the right. Some attendants stood behind the sofa. The other Moslems sat on low cushions close to the wall of the Durbar on either side, and by the uniformity of their white muslin robes, made an advantageous show. A glass door flanked our sofa. The curtain which covered it on the inside was every moment partially withdrawn; so that I imagine the Begum and other women were gratifying their curiosity. The Nawab said that the expressions I had used to him the day before had been balm to him; for that in his situation, he must unavoidably be anxious upon every change in the Government. He requested that I would look at the letters which he had received from the King and the Court of Directors on his accession to the Musnud, as well as at one from Lord Cornwallis. Having perused them, I said that my language had not been unweighed; for, that the existence of a specific Treaty would have bound me to strict observance of what I found so settled, even had the greatest political difference reigned between me and those who made the arrangement. I felt pledged to that principle of duty, and to the fulfilment of its true spirit of personal honour. He appeared overjoyed, and asked whether I wished to have his two sons under my eye at Calcutta, as Lord Cornwallis had had the children of Tippoo. I answered, that the case was widely different between a vanquished enemy and the representative of a family which had always preserved the most faithful alliance; and added, that nothing should induce me ever to give a colour for others to imply a doubt which I myself could not for an instant entertain."*

(C.)
(Page 122.)

The *Gwalior Gazette* contains the following Proclamation by H. H. the Maharajah Scindia upon the subject of the famine now prevailing in the North West.

TRANSLATED PROCLAMATION.—Issued by the Government of His Highness the Maharajah Alijah Jyajee Rao Scindia Bahadoor, G.C.S.I., dated Gwalior, the 9th September, 1868.

Whereas, by reason of the drought this year, the crops have failed and famine has come upon the land, in consequence of which the people, it is reported, are leaving their homes in vast numbers to emigrate to other and more favoured regions; and considering the disastrous effect of such migrations, equally to the State whose villages are thereby left deserted, to the people individually who become demoralised by the temptations presented by actual want, and to the general tranquillity of the country, from roving bands of desperate men; the Government of His Highness the Maharajah Scindia has resolved to adopt extraordinary measures of relief and precaution, to meet the emergency as dictated, equally in the interest of his subjects, and by considerations of a far-seeing economy.

Accordingly it is hereby notified for the information of the public generally, and more especially of lumberdars, putwaries, zemindars, canoongoes, potails, chowdries, and others interested, That having regard to the welfare of the people and in order to maintain them in unimpaired prosperity during the present season of drought, the collection of the first instalment of the Government revenue for the current year has been postponed in the affected districts.

It is notified further, that the ordinary precedure of the Courts

* Private Journal of the Marquis of Hastings, (1858) vol. ii, p. 11.

has been suspended temporarily, in respect of summonses for the attendance of parties in pending suits, whether as principals or witnesses, so that none may be put to unnecessary expense or trouble at this season of scarcity and distress.

The village authorities above named are therefore enjoined to remain at home in peace and quietness with their respective village communities, and they are hereby authorised to promise on the part of the State, subsistence to all, either direct from the Government or through their respective bankers, on the guaranty of the State hereby given, until means can be devised for employing the people on public works of utility and grace.

Further to guard against danger from without, in the form of emigrants from other parts entering the Gwalior territories, Chiefs holding jaghires on the frontiers, are hereby directed to take the field and keep the border marches. All extra expenses attendant on this duty will be defrayed by the State.

His Highness's Government will watch carefully the effect of this Proclamation throughout the country. They entertain a confident assurance that the proofs herein exhibited of the paternal solicitude and liberality of the Government, cannot fail, if judiciously placed before the people, to retain them at their homes in resigned contentment, patiently waiting for better times. Hence the degree in which the inhabitants may stay or go, will be held to be the measure of the zeal and capacity of the respective district officials. His Highness's Government trusts them. Let all strive to justify this confidence.

By order of the Maharajah.

(Signed) GUNPUT RAO KURKEY,

Dewan of the Gwalior State.

The *Hindoo Patriot*, a Calcutta weekly paper, conducted entirely by Natives, has the following remarks on this Proclamation:—

"What a commentary is the above on the Famine policy of the British Government in Orissa! In what striking and noble contrast is it to the recent Resolution of the Government on the scarcity in Upper India. In the case of Orissa, after petitioning for months, continued agitation in the press, half-a-dozen local inquiries, and the depopulation of hundreds of villages, the zemindars and the ryots obtained the remission of only one kist" (instalment). "Even in the recent Resolution, remission has been enjoined in such cautious terms that it will, we fear, be practically neutralised in the hands of over zealous local officers. Then in the Gwalior Proclamation, a general order has been issued upon the 'village authorities' 'to promise on the part of the State subsistence to all, either direct from the Government or through their respective bankers, on the guaranty of the State, until means can be devised for employing the public on public works of utility and grace." This is a sort of liberality which only Native Princes can exercise. It passes, we fear, the comprehension of a European statesman, tied down as he is by the stiff rules of political economy. The vastness of the organisation necessary for such a stupendous work, baffles his imagination. The Natives of India, accustomed to feed thousands *en masse*, entertain, however, a different estimate of such work. The closing of the Courts during the continuance of the famine is characteristic. When the people have not means to live they cannot afford to litigate. We shall watch with great interest the practical operation of the Resolution of the Gwalior Government."

In another part of the same article there is this passage :—

"Much as we admire the liberality of our own Government, we feel a pride in the statesmanship and large-heartedness which the Gwalior State has displayed in dealing with the same calamity within its territories."

And we read as follows in the news-columns of the same paper :—

"The Native Princes are behaving nobly in reference to the impending scarcity in their territories. The Maharajah of Jeypore, we are told, has exempted all grain from duty. He loses about Rs. 120,000 this year by the measure."

(D).
PRIVATE ACCOUNTS OF THE LATE MAHARAJAH OF MYSORE.
(Page 127.)

On the 23rd of July, 1868, the *Friend of India* announced with great exultation, that since the death of the Maharajah of Mysore some important disclosures had been made by an examination of his private accounts. "The accounts of the late Maharajah," he continues, "are now before the Government of India, *we believe*." For the present he confines himself to one disclosure. "Major Evans Bell appears in the books as the recipient of some 10,000 rupees, while publishing the most violent and professedly disinterested attacks, not only on the policy of the Government, but on individuals."

All this is very wide of the mark. It would be much more to the purpose, if he would allege, as the preliminary to proof that my " attacks" were unjust, unfair, or groundless. My 'violence"—if there was any,—can only have impaired my arguments. " Disinterestedness,"—whether professed or not,—cannot have added weight to my advocacy, or have contributed in any degree to a successful result.

This demand for " disinterested" advocacy seems to be considered very effective at Calcutta, for in a letter which must have been written about the same time in his capacity of " Our Own Correspondent," printed in the *Times* of the 24th August, 1868, the same person tells the story of the Mysore private accounts, " which have lately come before the Government of India since the Maharajah's death," and, without mentioning my name or any other name, declares that they " reveal the extent to which the old man's enormous income, and the large sums which *we* more than once gave him to pay his debts,"—his own money, as explained at p. 112—13,—" were squandered" in agitating his claims. He then adds: " It was essential to the success of these agitators that they should be believed to be disinterested." If by " disinterested" he means, as I suppose, *unpaid*, greater nonsense was never penned. The success of the Rajah's appeal could not have been in the least advanced by any such belief. The case of the Rajah of Mysore depended, and was decided, on its merits, not on any " belief" in the personal merits or private means of its advocates. None but a corrupt or imbecile judge would give any weight to such considerations.

The Editor of the *Friend of India*, after bringing equally well founded charges against me of " concealment," " pretended disinterestedness," and " outrageous plagiarism," concludes by triumphantly asking me, " What about those ten thousand rupees ?"

He is very much mistaken if he thinks that these " revelations" and " disclosures" can at all disturb my equanimity. Personally I am quite indifferent to the very questionable procedure of the Calcutta Foreign Office. The mere fact that some of the expenses incurred by me had been covered by a donation from the Rajah, —that I had at last accepted a brief in a cause which I had for years pleaded gratuitously,—was no secret to my friends, or to any one who had occasion to inquire. The following extract from the *Saturday Review* of March 2nd, 1867, will prove that there was no great mystery in the matter :—" The history of Mysore has been told in a spirited volume by Major Evans Bell, who, after urging on public grounds the restoration of the Native Sovereignty, has now, since his retirement from the service, become the avowed agent or advocate of the Rajah."

I never was, properly speaking, the *agent* of the Rajah,—that is to say, I never had any credentials or instructions; I never was entrusted with funds, or had any control over expenditure. I began to work at this case without any communication with the Rajah, at my own discretion, and by my own resources, continuing, in fact, at home, the course I had pursued for several years before leaving India. I should, under any circumstances, have done all I could to promote the restoration of Mysore as a Native State, dealing with the case, as I have always done, not as the grievance of an individual, but as part and parcel of a great scheme of Imperial policy. If I had been left entirely to my own resources, I could not have done so much, but I should still have done my best.

So long as I was in public employ I wrote and published—sometimes anonymously in periodicals, sometimes under my own name,—with no idea of pay or profit. All who know me, all who choose to inquire, know that my opinions on Indian politics have not been recently adopted, but that I have held them, and taken every opportunity of spreading them, for the last thirteen years. I did not want a Rebellion to teach me the mischief and danger of a rapacious policy. In 1855, I attacked Lord Dalhousie in the *Delhi Gazette*. Early in 1859 my letters on the Rebellion, which had appeared during the two preceding years in the London *Daily News* and *Leader*, were reprinted in a volume called "The English in India," and will be found not to differ in the least in principle and tendency from what I have written since that time. The same may be said of my contributions to the *Times of India*, the Madras *Athenæum*, and the *Indian Statesman*, down to 1863, when I returned home.

In April, 1861, an article in the *Indian Statesman* from my pen, (reprinted in 1864 in my book "The Empire in India,") recommended the very policy towards Mysore,—the maintenance of the State under an adopted heir, and the gradual restoration of Native agency,—which has lately been ordered by the Secretary of State to be carried out in every particular.

The Editor of the *Friend of India* says, stupidly enough, that I made "attacks on the policy of Government." The Government has actually carried out the policy that I upheld for seven years, and has rejected the policy that I attacked. The Mysore Rajah's right to adopt an heir and successor to his Principality, vehemently denied at Calcutta, was so incontrovertible when the case was once put into shape, that in a very full House of Commons on the 22nd of February, 1867, scarcely a dissentient murmur was heard when Lord Cranborne announced his determination to cancel the repeated decisions of the Viceroy, and to recognise the adopted son. If I preached false doctrine, adverse to the interests of the Empire, so have Her Majesty's Ministers, and the Lords and Commons have acquiesced in it.

The tone and temper with which the executive functionaries in India have received the news of their defeat,—the manner in which, like their organ, they habitually speak of themselves as " the Government,"—betray very clearly how unwilling they are to be restricted to their legitimate duties of administering the affairs of India under the control and instructions of the British Crown and Parliament. They unwittingly arrogate to themselves every Imperial prerogative. They resent the effective interference of the Home authorities, and object to any information or opinion on Indian affairs being conveyed to the Secretary of State except through the medium of their despatches and "collections." They have yet to learn the first principles of the Imperial constitution, and their place in its practical working.

Reasonable persons, free from the official trammels and prejudices of Indian service, will admit that there may be political cases beyond the cognisance of any municipal court, where a Native Prince has a right to appeal to the Crown and people of Great Britain against the erroneous or prejudiced verdict of provincial authority. Such a case was that of the Mysore Rajah's claims.

If then the Rajah of Mysore had a right to appeal, he had a right to secure competent advocates. If the work was lawful, surely payment was lawful. In many cases work is impossible without payment. Even the ultra Puritans of Calcutta (who, we may presume, never accept payment for their labour), would, perhaps, hesitate to push their notions of " disinterestedness" so far as to insist that no payment should be accepted for the expenses of printing, advertising, postage, carriage of parcels, travelling, the preparation of petitions, the purchase of books, and other essential matters, which soon swallow up hundreds of pounds.

It is well known that more than one political appeal has been carried to a successful result by the well-paid exertions of solicitors, barristers, and parliamentary agents. I really cannot understand why I could not with as perfect propriety receive payment—or rather compensation,—for advocating the claims of the Rajah of Mysore, as could Sir Richard Bethell, then Her Majesty's Attorney General, for advocating the claims of the Ranee of Tanjore against the Government of India, when he denounced its policy as "most violent and unjustifiable." The only difference that I can see, is that the Attorney General must have received his fee before the appeal came on for hearing, while I received an unsolicited *quiddam honorarium*, when the greater part of my voluntary work was done.

It may be said, such work is lawful for a professional advocate or agent, but not for a retired Indian officer in the receipt of a pension. Why not? My half-pay does not bind me to political apathy or quiescence, or deprive me of the rights of a citizen. I owe no allegiance to Governors or Councillors. When out of employ I owe no obedience to any of them. By opposing the officials in power in one of our dependencies I am not opposing the Government, though for the matter of that I have the right of being in opposition if I choose.

Many eminent barristers, including some who have sat upon the woolsack, have been in the receipt of Army or Navy half-pay during the whole of their forensic career. I have never heard that any such person felt himself debarred from holding a brief against Government. Nor should I consider my position legally or morally modified, or my freedom of action increased, if I were now to be called to the bar. If half-pay or pension can be regarded as at all in the nature of a retaining fee, it ought to be as a retaining fee from the people who pay the revenue from which it is drawn, and not from the Executive Government for the time being.

Only one restriction appears to me morally binding upon a retired public servant. He has no right to make use of official information which he has acquired as a public servant, for the purpose of opposing or obstructing the Government which he formerly served, or, indeed, for any purpose whatever. Such information is not his property, nor is it at his disposal. The formal permission of Government is required for the publication of intelligence acquired under such circumstances. This rule I have never broken. I have sought for authentic information in every quarter: I have never published anything that came into my hands in any official capacity.

But this restriction is at least equally binding upon officials who have *not* retired. They have no right to make use of intelligence that falls into their hands officially, either for their private purposes, or for the attack or defence of public departments, without express permission.

Few breaches of confidence can be conceived more unwarrantable—not to say dishonourable,—than for an executor or trustee, placed in possession of the private accounts and correspondence of a deceased Prince or nobleman, to publish extracts from his letters, or detached items from his accounts, with the sole and express purpose of vilifying or annoying a political opponent, or a literary antagonist. This offence has been perpetrated, or permitted, by the Calcutta Foreign Office, with the magnanimous object of injuring the writer who pens these lines, and who has been openly attacking its distinctive policy,—not, perhaps, without effect—during the last four years.

Undoubtedly it became the duty of our Government, at the death of the late Rajah of Mysore, to take charge of all his property, and to have his private accounts and papers carefully searched and put in order, so that all sums due might be recovered, no false claims admitted, and no loss or malversation occur during the minority of the young Prince, our Ward. But our Government, acting as Guardian of a Native Prince, has no right to publish his private affairs, or those of his father, to the world.

With a view to putting a better face on this discreditable proceeding, it has been represented as the publication of some facts from "*the Secret-service accounts of the Mysore State.*" If this were true, the publication would still, unless expressly authorised by the Viceregal Government, be a breach of official trust. But it is not true. The affairs of "*the Mysore State*" were entirely in the hands of the British Commissioner. The Rajah's own affairs were strictly personal. The Rajah's private accounts referred solely to the receipts and disbursements of his privy purse, and concerned his family alone. British officials could demand access to them only in the confidential capacity of Guardian, and any knowledge thus obtained was available, in honour and justice, only for the protection and profit of the minor Prince.

It appears possible, as has been quite lately suggested to me, that the items of intelligence referred to in the text, may have been furnished to the *Friend of India* by an official not so highly placed as the Viceroy or the Foreign Secretary. It may be so, but if it could be shown to be so beyond a doubt, a great deal more would have to be shown before the aspect of the transaction was altered to the credit or honour of the Viceregal Government. It would have to be shown that the Viceroy, on learning the publication of those items of intelligence, knowing well from whom they must have proceeded, had promptly disavowed and rebuked the unwarrantable breach of confidence committed by his subordinate, and had done his best to counteract and contradict the mischievous impression that the *Friend of India*, the vehicle for that breach of confidence, is the favoured organ of Government. Nothing of this sort has ever, to my knowledge, been done.

(E.)
EXTRACTS FROM THE TIMES AND PALL MALL GAZETTE.
(Page 154.)

From the TIMES, October 10, 1868.

"There is a case now under the final consideration of the India Office—that of Prince Azeem Jah, which, though often discussed in India, is comparatively unknown at home. One or two Parliamentary debates a few sessions back gave it, indeed, a transient political importance, but it is now again almost forgotten. We have at present no wish to revive its history or to inflict at length upon our readers its somewhat dry details. Indeed, we refer to it partly in order to express our hope that it may at length be finally settled after so many years of wearisome, wasteful mismanagement, and that Parliament and the press may not again be troubled with it—a dreary contingency which is, unhappily, still possible. But before it passes away into the cold oblivion of ancient Indian history, and is handed over by political departments to students and antiquaries, there is one feature about it that we think well worth a passing notice, from the curious and instructive light which it throws upon official affairs in India, and specially upon the popular theory of Anglo-Indian 'administrative capacity.' This feature, stripped of surroundings, is briefly this —that having long ago pledged themselves to relieve Prince Azeem Jah from the pressure of his debts and to pacify his creditors, the Indian authorities have managed the task in such an extraordinary way that at the present moment they have not only failed entirely to accomplish it, but have actually increased the importunity of the more important creditors, and, as a consequence, the troubles of the Prince. Yet the task was by no means a difficult one, and the rock upon which it has been wrecked was one which it needed no political prescience or penetration to avoid. A little common sense, combined with the most ordinary knowledge of human nature, was all that was required. The Prince's creditors formed two very different classes; one class, the 'secured,' having great powers of annoying him—by selling his mortgaged property, and arresting the friends who had gone security for him; the other, or 'unsecured,' having no such means whatsoever, being dependent entirely on the promise of the Prince, who is himself above the jurisdiction of the law courts, and exempt from arrest. Now, as the main object of the authorities was to relieve the Prince—who had, in return, pledged himself to cease from all agitation for what he had previously claimed as his ancestral rights—it would have seemed that the one fact which above all others they ought to have kept prominently in view was this vital all-important distinction between the two classes of creditors.

"For some inscrutable reason, however, they either could not or would not see this, but resolved to treat all the creditors in precisely the same way. They appointed a Commissioner to examine all claims and to distribute the Government grant, but at the same time formally stipulated that any creditor who brought a claim before the Commissioner should, merely by so doing, resign all right whatsoever further to sue or solicit the Prince, no matter whether the Commissioner accepted the claim or not. The natural, we might almost say the necessary, consequence of this extraordinary measure was that only the 'unsecured' creditors accepted the polite but precarious invitation. As they never had any means of putting pressure on the Prince, they did not care if the Commissioner rejected their claims; their hold on the Prince remained practically just what it was before—a matter for his free consideration; while, on the other hand, if their claims were even in part accepted, they got some Government money. But the 'secured' creditors, having a firm hold on the Prince, of course declined to run the grave risk incurred by thus putting themselves entirely at the mercy of the Commissioner. They failed to see the advantage of giving up everything on the chance of getting nothing. They left the Government grant, £150,000, to the 'unsecured' creditors, upon whom it is, to all practical purposes, utterly wasted, since paying them in no way 'relieves the Prince,' and they themselves set to work to badger him more vigorously than ever, very nearly creating a serious riot among the Mussulman population of Madras by attempting to arrest one of his sons in the harem. The Indian authorities are, accordingly, after years of worry and of the most wasteful expenditure of money and 'administrative capacity,' much further from their object than when they began. Not only are the Prince's creditors more troublesome than ever, but his debts—some of them chargeable with such enormous interest as sixty per cent.—have been increasing like a rolling snowball, to say nothing of the expense of the ingenious Commission itself. It is rumoured that they now, with almost equal ingenuity, have devised a scheme for paying the secured creditors with money stopped out of the Prince's revenues. In other words, they wish to take money out of his left pocket and put it into his right. If this clever conjuror's trick pleases him, well and good. As British taxpayers we shall not complain. But if he is not quite so simple, then we fear there will be further agitation of his claims, more wearisome talking in Parliament, more wearisome writing in the press, and, worse still, there will be the keeping still longer open one of those 'running sores' always so mischievous, sometimes at a crisis so dangerous, to the contentment and consequent prosperity of our Indian Empire. Let us hope to be spared this further proof of Anglo-Indian 'administrative capacity.'"

From the *Pall Mall Gazette*, 28th August, 1868.

"The Prince's debts were of two very different kinds, called respectively 'secured' and 'unsecured.' As the names imply, the former were those for which the creditors had some security in the shape of a claim either upon the property of the Prince himself, or upon the property, and also the persons, of his guarantees. These creditors had accordingly almost unlimited means of annoying him, and, as we have seen, exercised them very freely. The other class of creditors—the "unsecured"—had nothing but the Prince's promise to pay, and, as he was personally exempt from the jurisdiction of the law courts, this promise gave them no power whatever of annoyance. Our readers must keep carefully in mind this all-important distinction between the two classes of creditors, for the whole how-not-to-do-it character of the story turns upon it. Now, if Government had intended to pay all creditors in full, it obviously would not have mattered how or in what order they paid them. 'Secured' and 'unsecured' would then have fared alike, and been alike appeased. But full payment happened to be altogether out of the question. No sane Government would have offered, no sane creditor would even have expected it. There are countries, less virtuous than our own, in which this understanding is common enough. In India, for instance, we remember once asking a tradesman—and he was an ultro-respectable Briton moreover, keeping more than one gig—how he protected himself from loss in dealing with Native Princes above the law? His method was very simple. He 'charged four times the value of the article, and made the purchaser pay half in advance.' The Government, in the case under discussion, made an approximate estimate not of what sum the creditors claimed, but of what was likely to quiet them, and straightway set about dividing it. A legislative Act was passed appointing a Commissioner—of course on a handsome salary,—and all creditors 'secured' and 'unsecured,' were told that if they would appear by a certain date before him he would, on the part of the Government, consider their claims to a share in the money voted for the Prince but—and the 'but' is all-important—it was further distinctly stipulated that, whether the Commissioner approved a claim or not, the claimant, by the mere act of bringing it before him, forfeited his right to enforce it on the Prince; in other words, the Commissioner, while binding himself to nothing, expected the creditors to bind themselves to everything : if their claims happened to be approved, well and good, they got more or less money ; but if not, they lost everything—they got no money from the Commissioner, and yet could not again turn to the Prince. Now surely, one would think, even the average official intellect might have foreseen the natural, the inevitable consequences of such a measure as this. You have a large body of creditors, of whom some have cogent means of enforcing their claims, while the rest have no means whatsoever, and though it is known and confessed that you are not going to pay the claims in full, or anything like in full, you ask all the creditors to put themselves on the same equal footing and accept just what they can get—much, little, or nothing, as you may think fit. Are not the consequences as certain as that the sun will rise to-morrow? The unsecured creditors who have no power of annoying the Prince will come forward readily enough—they have nothing to lose, and everything to gain; but the secured will not voluntarily abandon their advantage ground, and come down to the level of the unsecured. They will only exert more vigorously than ever the power of annoy-

N

ance which has already extorted from Government some concessions, in the hope that it will extort more.

"However, the official intellect could not see all this. The Government undertook to relieve the Prince from duns and debt. The duns were never so troublesome and furious as they have been since the establishment of the commission; the debts have increased enormously, not unnaturally, considering that they all bear interest, some of them as high as sixty per cent. It undertook to do justice to the creditors, going out of its way, sacrificing its main object, in order to avoid favouring one class of creditors at the expense of the other. It has really handed over to one class the money intended for both, since, according to the lawyers, the 'unsecured' creditors, having alone complied with the conditions prescribed by Government, are alone entitled to the money voted by it. It undertook, by a satisfactory settlement of the Prince's affairs, to rid itself of a standing source of odium and embarrassment. It still has the Prince lying more helplessly than ever on its hands, with heavier debts and more rabid duns; and, in addition to this, having given him a new title, to be continued to his family, it bids fair to present to its subjects the edifying spectacle of a line of Princes of its own creation hopelessly bankrupt and beggared. It undertook to conciliate the large class of Natives, naturally discontented and disgusted at the misfortunes of their dethroned Prince. It had the satisfaction the other day of seeing a serious riot, occasioned by the attempt of a bailiff to force his way into the women's apartments, and arrest the Prince's son. If another bailiff would only succeed in getting into the harem, and insulting two or three ladies of the family, Government might even have, perhaps, the pleasure of putting down a little Mutiny. It undertook—but why multiply needless proofs of this unrivalled power of not doing a thing? It is more to the point to warn the circumlocutionists not to be lulled into a false security by their brilliant success. There are rumours that another sum of money—we believe £100,000 or £150,000—is likely to be voted for distribution among the 'secured' creditors. If by any supineness or inadvertence on the part of the circumlocutionists this sum be allowed to reach its destination, the creditors may be appeased; the Prince relieved, Government disembarrassed, and the people pleased: in a word, the toilsome work and glorious monument of years may be overthrown in a day.

"It now only remains for us to tell the general reader who the personages of our story are. He will hear with a thrill of patriotic pride what, unless he is a very vainglorious Briton, he will of course never have ventured to suspect—that the gifted circumlocutionists are his own fellow-countrymen, and may be seen any day in Victoria-street, Calcutta, and Madras. The Prince is that illustrious Nawab, or ex-Nawab, of the Carnatic, and scarcely less illustrious Parliamentary bore, his Highness AZEEM JAH."

(F).
Essential parts of the Treaties, with an Extract from an Opinion by the Honourable J. B. Norton, now Advocate General and Member of the Legislative Council of Madras.

Preamble to the Treaty of 1787.

"Treaty of perpetual friendship, alliance, and security, concluded between the Honourable Major-General Sir Archibald Campbell, Knight of the Bath, President and Governor of Fort St. George and the Council thereof, on the part of the United Company of Merchants trading to the East Indies, and His Highness the Nawab Wallajah Omdut-ool-Moolk Ameer-ool-Hind Asoph-ood-Dowlah Anwar-ood-deen Khan Bahadoor Zaffer Jung Sipah Salar, Soobadar of the Carnatic, on behalf of himself, *his heirs and successors."**

From the Preamble to the Treaty of 1792.

"The Right Honourable Charles Earl Cornwallis, Knight of the Most Noble Order of the Garter, Governor General, &c., &c., &c., invested with full powers on the part of the Honourable English East India Company, *their heirs and successors, on one part*, and the Nawab Wallajah Ameer-ool-Hind Omdut-ool-Moolk Asoph-ood-Dowlah Anwar-ood-deen Khan Bahadoor Zaffer Jung Sipah Salar, Nawab of the Carnatic, in his own name, and for himself and his successor, his eldest son, the Nawab Omdut-ool-Oomra, and *his heirs and successors, on the other part*, agree to the following Articles, which shall be binding on the respective *contracting parties."†*

TREATY with AZEEM-OOD-DOWLAH, 1801.

"Treaty for settling the succession to the Soubadarry of the territories of Arcot, and for vesting the administration of the civil and military government of the Carnatic Payen Ghat in the United Company of Merchants of England trading to the East Indies.

* *Collection of Treaties*, vol. v, p. 227.
† *Ibid.*, vol. v. p. 236.

"Whereas the several Treaties which have been concluded between the United Company of Merchants of England trading to the East Indies, and their Highnesses heretofore Nawabs of the Carnatic, have been intended to cement and identify the interests of the contracting parties; and whereas, in conformity to the spirit of the alliance, the said Company did, by the Treaty concluded on the 12th July, 1792, with the late Nawab Wolau Jah, relinquish extensive pecuniary advantages, acquired by the previous Treaty of 1787, with the view and on the consideration of establishing a more adequate security for the interests of the British Government in the Carnatic; and *whereas subsequent experience has proved that the intention of the contracting parties has not been fulfilled by the provisions of any of the Treaties heretofore concluded between them;* and whereas the musnud of the Soubadarry of Arcot having become vacant, the Prince Azeem-ood-Dowlah Bahadoor has been established by the English East India Company in the rank, property, and possessions of his ancestors, heretofore Nawabs of the Carnatic; and whereas the said Company and His Highness the said Prince Azeem-ood-Dowlah Bahadoor have judged it expedient that *additional provisions should at this time be made for the purpose of supplying the defects of all former engagements, and of establishing the connection between the said contracting parties on a permanent basis of security, in all times to come;* wherefore the following Treaty is now established and concluded by the Right Honourable Edward Lord Clive, Governor in Council of Fort St. George, by and with the sanction and authority of His Excellency the Most Noble the Marquis Wellesley, K. P., Governor General in Council of all the British possessions in the East Indies, on behalf of the said United Company, on the one part, and by His Highness the Nawab Wolau Jah Ummeer-ool-Dowlah Madar-ool-Moolk Ummeer-ool-Hind Azeem-ool-Dowlah Bahadoor Showkut Jung Sippa Salar, Nawab Soubadar of the Carnatic, on his own behalf, on the other part, for settling the succession to the Soubadarry of the territories of Arcot, and for vesting the administration of the civil and military government of the Carnatic in the United Company of Merchants of England trading to the East Indies."

ARTICLE 1.

" The Nawab Azeem-ood-Dowlah Bahadoor is hereby formally established in the state and rank, with the dignities dependent thereon, of his ancestors, heretofore Nawabs of the Carnatic, and the possession thereof is hereby guaranteed by the Honourable East India Company to His said Highness Azeem-ood-Dowlah Bahadoor, who has accordingly succeeded to the Soubadarry of the territories of Arcot."

APPENDIX. 181

ARTICLE 2.

" *Such parts of the Treaties heretofore concluded between the said East India Company and their Highnesses, heretofore Nawabs of the Carnatic, as are calculated to strengthen the alliance, to cement the friendship, and to identify the interests of the contracting parties, are hereby renewed and confirmed,* and accordingly the friends or enemies of either are the friends and enemies of both parties.

ARTICLE 3.

"The Honourable Company hereby charges itself with the maintenance and support of the military force necessary for the defence of the Carnatic, and for the protection of the rights, person, and property of the said Nawab Azeem-ood-Dowlah Bahadoor; *and with the view of reviving the fundamental principles of the alliance between his ancestors and the English Nation,* the said Nawab Azeem-ood-Dowlah stipulates and agrees that he will not enter upon any negociation or correspondence with any European or Native Power, without the knowledge and consent of the said English Company.

ARTICLE 4.

" It is hereby stipulated and agreed that the sole and exclusive administration of the civil and military governments of all the territories and dependencies of the Carnatic Payen Ghat, together with the full and exclusive right to the revenues thereof (with the exception of such portion of the said revenues as shall be appropriated for the maintenance of the said Nawab and for the support of his dignity) shall be for ever vested in the said English Company; and the said Company shall *accordingly* possess the sole power and authority of constituting and appointing *without any interference on the part of the said Nawab,* all officers for the collection of the revenues, and of establishing Courts for the administration of civil and criminal judicature.

ARTICLE 5.

" It is hereby stipulated and agreed that one-fifth part of the net revenues of the Carnatic shall be annually allotted for the maintenance and support of the said Nawab and of his own immediate family.* * *

ARTICLE 9.

" The English Company engages to take into consideration the actual situation of the families of their Highnesses the late Nawabs Wolau Jah and Omdut-ool-Omrah Bahadoor, as well as the situation of the principal officers of His late Highness's government; and the British Government shall charge itself with the expense (chargeable on the revenues of the Carnatic) of a suitable provision for their respective maintenance. The amount of the above-mentioned expenses, to be defrayed by the Company, *shall be distributed, with the knowledge of the said Nawab, in such manner as shall be judged proper.*

ARTICLE 10.

"The said Nawab Azeem-ood-Dowlah Bahadoor shall, in all places, on all occasions, and at all times, be treated with the respect and attention due to His Highness's rank and situation, as an Ally of the British Government, and a suitable guard shall be appointed from the Company's troops for the protection of His said Highness's person and palace.

*　　　　*　　　　*　　　　*　　　　*

SEPARATE EXPLANATORY ARTICLES.

"Separate Explanatory Articles annexed to the Treaty for settling the succession to the Soubadarry of the territories of Arcot and for vesting the administration of the civil and military government of the Carnatic Payen Ghat in the United Company of Merchants of England trading to the East Indies.

ARTICLE 1.

"Whereas it is stipulated by the fifth Article of the Treaty that the sum to be appropriated to the support of the dignity of His Highness the Nawab Azeem-ool-Dowlah Bahadoor shall be calculated at one-fifth part of the net revenues of the Carnatic, and whereas the improvement of the said revenues which, under Providence, may be expected to arise from the effects of the present arrangement, may render the said fifth part greater than will be necessary to the purposes intended by the contracting parties, it is hereby explained, for the better understanding of the 5th Article of the Treaty, that whenever the whole net revenue of the Carnatic, including the sums to be deducted, according to the 6th Article of the Treaty, shall exceed the sum of twenty-five lakhs of Star Pagodas, then in that case the fifth part of such surplus shall be applied to the repair of fortifications, to the establishment of a separate fund for the eventual exigencies of war, or to the military defence of the Carnatic, in such manner as may be determined by the Governor in Council of Fort St. George, *after previous communication to His Highness the Nawab Azeem-ood-Dowlah.*"*

* *Collection of Treaties*, vol. v., pp. 248 to 255.

Extract from the Opinion of Mr. J. B. Norton, now Advocate-General of Madras.

" Both Lord Harris and Lord Dalhousie insinuate a doubt as to whether the Treaty of 1801 can be considered a Treaty at all. This I presume is on the ground that the whole power was in the hands of the one party, the other entirely at his mercy.
" But the very first word in the contract is *'Treaties.'* Treaties are divided into *equal* and *unequal;* and they may be so either with regard to the status of the contracting parties, or the subject matter; and a Treaty is not less a Treaty because of the inequality of the parties, however that may differ in degree. Though Prince Azeem-ood-Dowlah was personally powerless, the condition of the country at that time, the comparatively unsettled power of the English, the chance of the Prince forming formidable alliances or combinations against them, were all ample consideration for their entering into a Treaty with him, as the next heir of the last tenant of the Musnud.
" Lord Harris in effect confines himself to the Treaty of 1801. Lord Dalhousie expressly says that 'it is *quite unnecessary* to *make any reference* to the Treaties of 1785, 1787, and 1792.'
" This is a very convenient and compendious fashion of getting rid of those Treaties; but the Treaty of 1801 is expressly *'for the purpose of supplying the defects of all former engagements;'* it refers to the Treaties of 1792 and 1787, which, it says, experience has proved not to have fulfilled their objects; and according to all the ordinary rules of interpretation, all these Treaties must necessarily be read together, and form in fact one Treaty.
" If this be so, there is an end of the question, for the earlier Treaties are all expressed to be with the Nabobs *'their heirs and successors,'* and from a perusal of them it will be seen that they are real Treaties, from the very objects they sought to provide for.
" The Treaty of 1801 provides *'additional'* provisions for supplying the *'defects'* of former engagements. How can these defects be ascertained, how can what is *additional* be defined, without a reference to the *former* Treaties?
" The 2nd Article of the Treaty of 1801 expressly ratifies, *'renews and confirms,'* all parts of former Treaties which are *'calculated to strengthen the alliance, cement the friendship, and identify the interests of the contracting parties.'*
" How can the earlier Treaties be repudiated in the face of this Article? What can be more calculated to effect these objects than those parts of the former Treaties which settle the order of succession to the Musnud, and make it perpetual in the reigning family—the very object of the Treaty of 1801 being ' to *settle* the succession' to the Carnatic?

"But I am further of opinion that the Treaty of 1801, taken by itself, is a real and not a personal Treaty.

"It is not necessary, as Grotius points out, that the term 'heirs and successors,' should be 'introduced in order to make the Treaty *real*.' It suffices if such terms are used as show it is not to be confined to a specified limited duration; and I find that the Treaty of 1801 expressly recites that it is 'to place the *connection* between the contracting parties on a *permanent* basis of security *in all time to come*.' How is this language possible, compatible with a severance of connexion immediately on the death of Azeem-ood-Dowlah? Article 4 vests the 'administration' of the Carnatic in the East India Company '*for ever*.' This is the other side of the contract; and surely the same duration must be given to the one as to the other.

"Looking at the acts of the East India Company when the Musnud was vacant in 1801, I cannot but think that what they really did was to re-establish it in the person of Azeem-ul-Dowlah *and his successors*.

"If the whole body of Treaties, as I think, form one Treaty, if the favourable parts of all former Treaties were *renewed* by the Treaty of 1801, there can be no doubt about it."

www.ingramcontent.com/pod-product-compliance
Lightning Source LLC
Chambersburg PA
CBHW032143160426
43197CB00008B/760